The KING of KINGS

The KING of KINGS

BRUCE D. PORTER

DESERET
BOOK®

Library of Congress Cataloging-in-Publication Data

Porter, Bruce D.
   The King of Kings / Bruce D. Porter.
     p. cm.
   Includes bibliographical references.
  ISBN 1-57345-886-4
      1. Jesus Christ—Mormon interpretations. 2. Atonement. 3. Christian life—Church of Jesus Christ of Latter-day Saints authors. I. Title

BX8643.J4 P67 2000
232'.3—dc21

           00-057064

Printed in the United States of America   54459-6705
10 9 8 7 6 5 4 3 2 1

Dedicated to my father and mother,
Lyle Kay Porter and Wilma Holmes Porter,
Goodly parents, deeply loved.

CONTENTS

PREFACE

This is a book that began as a letter. In the spring of 1997, medical reasons necessitated my return to the United States from Frankfurt, Germany, where I had been serving in the Europe East Area Presidency of The Church of Jesus Christ of Latter-day Saints. My family was not able to join me immediately. When I learned that they would be able to come to Salt Lake City on Easter Sunday, I set out to write my children an Easter letter about the Savior and his Atonement. That letter, with some revisions, became the first chapter of this book. The writing of that letter kindled in me a desire to learn and share more about the Savior, his life, and mission. The result, three years later, is this short volume.

The King of Kings is foremost my individual witness and testimony of Jesus Christ. Although it contains doctrinal commentary and many scriptures, I did not conceive it primarily as a doctrinal work. There is much here that is personal and from the heart. The book reflects my own views and opinions only and does not necessarily represent the official doctrines or viewpoints of The Church of Jesus Christ of Latter-day Saints. While I have tried to be orthodox and doctrinally correct in every point, any errors are entirely my own responsibility.

I owe a special debt of gratitude to my wife, Susan, and my children, David, Chris, Lisa, and Jennifer, who have supported me in this endeavor, as well as in my calling as a Seventy, with much patience and love. Susan read all the chapters in draft form and offered many valuable comments. I am also very appreciative of my sister, Pamela Hamblin, an outstanding editor and wordsmith who read every chapter carefully and offered extensive editorial suggestions. The board, editors, and staff of Deseret Book have given excellent counsel and support in every way. Particular thanks goes to Cory Maxwell, director of the Deseret Book imprint, who encouraged me from the beginning and provided many helpful comments. I would also like to thank Janna DeVore, who edited the manuscript and worked tirelessly to bring it to publication.

My parents, Lyle Kay and Wilma Holmes Porter, instilled in me a testimony of Jesus Christ and his Church from an early age. They have been models of Christlike living, whose examples have blessed me throughout my life. Gratefully, this book is dedicated to them.

CHAPTER ONE
AN EASTER LETTER

Salt Lake City, Utah
April 1997

My dear children,

In only six days it will be Easter. As if in anticipation, a gentle breeze is flowing from the canyons through the valley, refreshing the air in its wake. The sky is desert blue, birds are exulting in song, and flowers are breaking forth in violet, yellow, and red. In all my life I cannot remember an Easter without sunshine, and the coming Sabbath looks to be another golden day. But believe me, children, not even the most miserable weather would diminish the joy I feel knowing that we will be together this Easter Sunday. I have missed you dearly since I became ill and had to leave our home in Frankfurt and come to Salt Lake City for medical treatment last month.

Often when we are separated, I bring you home a gift. This Easter I wish to share with you a gift that cannot be purchased with money, a gift of greater worth than any inheritance of wealth. This priceless gift is the knowledge and testimony of Jesus Christ, the Anointed One, whose victory over death we celebrate on Easter Day. I want you to know and love, as I do, this humble carpenter from Nazareth who is also the King of

1

Creation, the Son of God, and the Redeemer of all mankind. This is why I am writing you an Easter letter. There is so much I desire to share about this man who was more than just a man. I hope you will read and ponder this letter more than once and someday share it with your children and grandchildren. If you can come to trust and love the Lord Jesus Christ with all your hearts, then I will have no fear whatsoever regarding your future. You will possess the one sure key to happiness, peace, and eternal life.

A wise seminary teacher and writer once wrote that Latter-day Saint parents often teach the gospel as though it were only a set of rules, standards, and "thou shalt nots," never clearly explaining *why* we should live the commandments, failing to introduce their children to the Law-Giver himself, not imparting to them a testimony and love of the Savior. I do not want to make that mistake. If we truly love God and Christ, the gospel becomes far more than just a set of rules. It becomes a fountain of living waters, the one true source of life and peace. I want you to drink of those living waters.

We have talked together about the Savior, his life and Atonement, many times in the past, yet I am afraid my teaching has sometimes been so doctrinal and even abstract as to seem distant from real life, or perhaps simply "preachy" and repetitive. I have taught you much *about* Christ, but now I want to be certain that you actually *know* him as a real person and *love* him as your Savior. This letter is simply my way of introducing to you the living Christ, our Friend and King.

Why is it so important to know him? In order that you may comprehend, let us consider the world in which we live.

The earth as we know it is both beautiful and terrible. As

the handiwork of God, it is glorious beyond expression, an ever-changing kaleidoscope of natural wonders. Whether frost-graced winter, scarlet autumn, or flourishing summertime, truly "The heavens declare the glory of God; and the firmament sheweth his handywork" (Psalm 19:1). I thrill at the privilege of living on earth. I rejoice to think that this glorious planet will be the inheritance of the humble followers of Christ, when the meek shall inherit the earth.

There is also much that is precious and worthwhile in human society: music and poetry, good food and pleasant company, hobbies and sports, Thanksgiving and Christmas. There is recreation, laughter, learning, giving, and myriad delights on every side. Whenever I am inclined to get down on the world or judge my own country and countrymen too harshly, I simply think of the many good neighborhoods in which we have lived and the choice neighbors we have had, both in and out of the Church. You have each enjoyed the companionship of good friends, and you have tasted much of wholesome sociality at school, home, and Church in your childhood years.

But we all know that there is a darker side. Notwithstanding its divine creation and eternal destiny, ours is a fallen world, an often terrible realm where darkness and evil find abundant place. The planet on which we live once stood near to the presence of God; filled with the transcendent light of his presence, it was a veritable garden place, a paradise unsullied. Then came the great Fall of Man, when darkness and death entered the world. It was essential that the Fall happen, for reasons we will discuss, but that necessity did not lessen the magnitude of the consequences. On every side we see iniquity, selfishness, hatred, envy, violence, betrayal, deceit, and crime. There is injury, illness, famine, plague, and death, sometimes early or painful death. There is poverty, terrorism, warfare, deception, oppression, and a million forms of pain and evil to rob our peace and destroy that which is good. And do not think that only the unrighteous experience the sorrows of this earth. Certainly if you live righteous lives, you will know more happiness than sorrow, but even the righteous are not spared from pain and bitter trial in this world. It is necessary for our experience and testing, and it is the inevitable fruit of a fallen world. No matter how good and carefully you live, you will witness a great deal that is sorrowful and evil, for we live in the latter days, when the powers of darkness are putting forth every possible energy to destroy the work of God.

Shortly before his martyrdom, the Prophet Joseph Smith said of the Latter-day Saints, "Little do they know the trials that await them." I would say the same to you. Great trials and challenges lie ahead in your lives. You will need every ounce of strength and righteousness to endure. But more than that, you will need the power and comfort of the Lord Jesus Christ in your life. You will need a Savior, a Support, a divine Friend, one who will protect you, stand by you, and make you strong in every hour of trouble. None other than Christ can do this for you.

Who is this Jesus Christ? History records that he was born of a peasant woman, Mary, in Bethlehem, and raised as a carpenter's son in Nazareth. His given name was *Joshua* or *Jeshua,* which in Greek, and later English, became *Jesus.* It was a common enough name in that day, yet its meaning—Jehovah is salvation—portended his messianic mission. Because Christ's birth in Bethlehem was largely hidden from the world, he was thought to be a Nazarene, and was known generally as Jesus of Nazareth. He was a woodworker most of his life, until, at about age thirty, he began a ministry of teaching, healing, and serving the Jewish people of Palestine. His ministry lasted a mere three years, during which time he taught such revolutionary doctrine and performed such marvelous miracles that his fame spread through all Judaea. He became a threat to the entrenched religious hierarchy of the day. Arrested on trumped-up charges of sedition, he was brought before the Roman authorities—who held ultimate political power in Palestine—and, under a tide of popular pressure, condemned to death. Crucified between two thieves, his life ended in seeming disgrace, with most of his followers abandoning him in the last desperate hours before his death. Only a few women and one trusted follower named John even dared to attend his execution.

Though his life was short and his end sudden, the power of his teachings and surpassing virtue of his daily life was such that he came to be recognized as the pivotal figure in human history, with the world's calendar itself divided by the year of his birth. Hundreds of millions have proclaimed themselves his followers throughout the ages. For Christians everywhere, he was indisputably the greatest man that ever lived, a model of virtue and holiness unsurpassed and unsurpassable.

I testify that he was indeed the greatest soul who ever walked the earth. He lived a perfect life in every point. That fact alone gives us ample reason to study his life and master his teachings. But his mortal life alone was only one part of what he represents. If we think of Jesus as only a great historical leader and teacher who lived nearly two thousand years ago, we will have missed the mark of truth by a wide margin. If his name brings to mind only images of ancient Palestine, the stormy sea of Galilee, the crowded stone streets of Jerusalem, or the cottages of Capernaum, then we will have hardly begun to understand who he was at all. For Jesus is far more than the man whose life is chronicled in the New Testament—vastly, infinitely more. Jesus of Nazareth was and is the Lord and King of all creation. As the LDS Bible Dictionary says under the heading "Christ": "He is Lord of lords, King of kings, the Creator, the Savior, the God of the whole earth, the Captain of our salvation, the Bright and Morning Star. He is in all things, above all things, through all things, and round about all things; he is Alpha and Omega, the first and the last; his name is above every name, and is the only name under heaven by which we can be saved."

Before this world was, we knew him. In the premortal life, when we lived with God the Father as spirit children, he stood among us as the Firstborn and Anointed of the Father, a Being of surpassing intelligence and light, whom we joyfully received as our Lord and leader. We knew him. We followed him. We adored him. He had become in every point like our Father in Heaven—though yet without a glorified body, and ever His loyal and obedient son. In that premortal realm, we embraced God's plan for our future and defended it zealously against the accusations and slander of Lucifer, his arch rival and bitter enemy.

You already know the story of that Grand Council in Heaven, the war with Lucifer and his hosts that followed, the grand plan of agency and salvation proposed and accepted by two-thirds of our Father's children. I will not review those events here. My point is simply this: though we have forgotten all, there was a time when we personally knew and loved Jesus as our Captain and Friend, a time when we esteemed him as the greatest of all, save only Father in Heaven himself. Our challenge now is to come to know him again and, through faith in him, to overcome the trials and temptations of this world and return to our Father's presence. He is the key to that celestial homecoming. In his own words, *"I am the door"* (John 10:9; emphasis added). The Door to eternal life, the Door to God's presence.

Without the Atonement of Christ, we would be consigned to everlasting exile from the presence of God. With no means for repentance available—no way to cleanse our spirits of the stain of sin—the accumulated effects of transgression would mount until we became captives of the adversary (2 Nephi 9:7–9). From the beginning, there was one and only one way to avoid this awful end—a perfect being would have to offer up his life as a sinless sacrifice for our sins. Moved by pure love, Christ in the Grand Council volunteered to ransom us from sin and death, to take upon himself the full penalty and payment of all the sins of mankind from Adam to the end of the world. That frightful burden—infinite in magnitude—would rest upon him alone. There was no other way. From before the creation of the world, all our hopes centered in him and his Atonement.

But why? you may ask. Why did God's Firstborn need to suffer and bear such an awful burden? Is not God all-powerful? Could he not simply decree that our sins were forgiven? For that matter, if God has the power to banish evil or prevent pain, why did he create a world in which both are so abundant? *If God is all-powerful, why do suffering and evil exist at all?*

That question has vexed philosophers and theologians for centuries. It troubles every human being who endures what he feels is a colossal injustice or an unbearable trial. When a family member is struck down by cancer, or a terrible crime destroys lives, or youth stray into forbidden paths despite every effort to save them, even the most faithful are tempted to ask: Why? Why did God allow this to happen? And if the trial is our own, we understandably cry out: Why did this have to happen to me? What have I done to deserve this? Why did not God prevent this from happening?

I have come to believe that the beginning of spiritual maturity is to understand that suffering and opposition are essential to the plan of redemption. Consider the penetrating insight of father Lehi: "For it must needs be, that there is an opposition in all things" (2 Nephi 2:11). This is among the most profound truths revealed in the Book of Mormon. Without sorrow, there could be no joy; without darkness, no light; without bitterness, no sweetness. The necessity of opposition is an eternal and unchangeable law, a law that permeates all of existence. Even the nature of physical matter illustrates this. Scientists now believe that no subatomic particle exists without a precise opposite particle—opposite in charge, spin, and other attributes. In everyday life, the law of opposition means that we must experience trial and adversity in order to know and appreciate joy and peace. We must overcome temptations in order to become strong. The slogan of many athletes, "no pain, no gain," may sound macho or trite, but it captures a fundamental reality of life.

We experience opposition from the moment of our birth, itself a traumatic experience whose physical stress helps prepare a newborn for the early rigors of life. Opposition continues through every moment and day of our existence. Much of the opposition we face is ordinary, and we think little of it. Take gravity, for example. Throughout our lives, our muscles must work to overcome the force of gravity and hold us upright. Every organ and cell of our body is affected by this force. Because of the subconscious effort we make to overcome it, our muscles and bodies develop and become strong. Astronauts, who during space travel are deprived for even short periods of this opposing force, experience the rapid atrophy of their muscles and organs. Every attempt to counter this degeneration, for example by physical exercise aboard the spacecraft, has only partly solved the problem, because no exercise can be designed that strains every cell and muscle of the body at every moment of time, as does gravity.

We take the opposing force of gravity for granted, of course. But the principle of opposition extends into all spheres of life, including the spiritual. Though God the Father has supreme power and could, in principle, banish Satan's influence entirely from the earth, he allows him and his legions to work here precisely in order that we may experience the forces of temptation, sin, and wickedness. Eliminate these from the equation of life, and we would never have opportunity to become strong spiritually, never would experience that victory over self that President David O. McKay called the essence of spirituality. A key purpose of our mortal existence—to learn to live righteously, even in the face of temptation and trial—would be defeated. The same is true of the sorrows and pains of life that are not linked directly with transgression, such as sickness, accidents, tragic deaths, and physical handicaps. Though difficult to bear, these are intended to test our faith, elicit our compassion, and magnify our spiritual understanding.

The principle of opposition in all things is intimately linked to the gift of moral agency granted to us in the grand plan of redemption. Without opposition, free choice would not exist. Adam and Eve fell from the presence of God—in accordance with divine intent—in order that their posterity might experience the opposition inherent in a fallen realm. Lucifer's world by contrast would have been a world without pain, sorrow, or sin. He would have used his power to banish all of these, eliminating human agency and turning the children of God into emotionless, soulless automatons—robots or pawns in his all-powerful grasp. What an awful vision! No one would have been lost, but nothing would have been gained either.

Lois Lowry's children's book, *The Giver*, describes a society from which all pain, all emotion, and all choice have been eliminated by careful planning and engineering. It is a society with no problems, no wars, no conflict, no failure or disappointment. Everything from birth to death is planned, manipulated, and controlled, like the working of a well-tuned clock. The consequence is a society without love, emotion, or beauty. Its inhabitants know no pain, because they have no feeling. They can perceive neither color nor beauty. Sensation itself is foreign to them. Their lives are the very definition of blandness. At the end of the novel, one young boy and his baby brother make a daring escape back into a world where injury, pain, and heartbreak are possible—back into a world of beauty, sensation, and freedom.

It is easy, of course, to talk and write about the necessity of opposition; it is far more difficult to experience it. Most of us, at some point in our lives, will face trials that seem unbearable. The piercing question—Why must this be?—may then still trouble us. The greatest of men have faced trials so heart-wrenching that they were led to cry out to God for understanding and relief. Joseph Smith, imprisoned for months in a dungeon at Liberty, Missouri, cried out: "O God, where art thou? And where is the pavilion that covereth thy hiding place?" (D&C 121:1). Even Jesus, at the pinnacle of his agony on the cross, was led to exclaim: "My God, my God, why hast thou forsaken me?" (Matthew 27:46). It is a cry echoed by the suffering throughout the ages.

If even the Savior agonized over partaking of the bitter cup, surely we must never judge those who struggle or waver under the burden of life's trials. We cannot know what pains or burdens others bear, and we may also someday experience trials that cause us to cry out in agony. There are no easy answers or cheap comforts for the supreme trials of life. But what I do know is this: in accepting the Father's plan in our premortal lives, we knowingly accepted that we would live in a world of pain, temptation, and constant trial. We accepted the possibility of great suffering and loss, even eternal loss. We knew that earth life would be very difficult at times and that many would fall from the truth. Yet we "shouted for joy" (Job 38:7) at the prospect of coming into this world. The freedom to choose—and thus to progress—meant that much to us.

There was another reason we rejoiced. Jesus, the author of

salvation, that Great Captain whom we loved so much, promised us that he would undergo the trials of earth life together with us. None of us would have to experience any pain or temptation that he would not also experience. Even death would lose its sting; for by virtue of his special station as the Only Begotten Son of the Father in the flesh, he would break open the portals of the grave and bring about the resurrection of every human being. Most glorious of all, he offered to take upon himself the entire burden of sin and guilt that would be the inevitable price of a world of agency. Despite the infinite suffering it would entail, he would ransom from sin all those who would repent of their sins, receive his ordinances, and accept him as their Savior. Is it any wonder, then, that we shouted for joy when the plan was proclaimed—joy no doubt mixed with adoration for the pure love and sacrifice of the great Redeemer?

Now I know that you have studied the importance of the Atonement in Sunday School, and seminary classes, and in discussions as a family. But perhaps there lingers yet some doubt or uncertainty in your hearts as to why it was necessary. The question I asked earlier must still be answered: Why could not God just decree our sins forgiven without any suffering on the part of Christ? Why did a ransom have to be made?

The answers to these questions may be found by prayerful pondering of the great discourses on the Atonement found in the Book of Mormon. While there are many passages of scripture touching on the Atonement, there are seven great discourses that stand apart as exceptional explications of that infinite event. I have in mind 2 Nephi 2; 2 Nephi 9; Mosiah 3–4; Mosiah 13–16; Alma 7; Alma 34; and Alma 42. I urge you to study and ponder these scriptures, and to make the study of the Atonement a matter of deep personal interest and commitment. But because I do not want to make this a doctrinal treatise, rather than reviewing these scriptures in detail, I am going to share with you a personal explanation distilled from my own study and meditation on the subject.

When we enter this world as infants, our spirits are pure and innocent. We remain innocent during the years of our childhood, but beginning at age eight, as our understanding of right and wrong develops, we become capable of committing sin. Because all of us are weak in some points, we all sin. Yet even a single sin, however small, makes us unworthy to return to the presence of God, "for no unclean thing can dwell there, or dwell in his presence" (Moses 6:57). Sin—all sin—opens up a vast, virtually infinite gulf between ourselves and our Father in Heaven, cutting us off from his presence. Every sin we commit also dims the brightness of our once innocent spirits, leaving a kind of spiritual stain on our souls—what I have sometimes heard called "earth stains." In our fallen state it is impossible to cleanse the stain of sin by our own power alone—hence, we remain cut off from the presence of God. Only a divine power can cleanse the stains from our souls, bridge the gulf between us and God, and give us strength to overcome temptation. This power, as Amulek explains so beautifully, must be "infinite and eternal" (Alma 34:14).

The Atonement of Jesus Christ is that infinite and eternal power. No other power can save us from our fallen state or free us from the fetters of sin. Christ's travail in Gethsemane and on the cross was literally infinite, in that he experienced the equivalent of every pain, sorrow, darkness, ordeal, and affliction that exists in the universe. He "descended below all things" (D&C 88:6). Only the Son of God, sinless and of divine birth, could have borne such an incomprehensible weight. In doing so, he fulfilled the demands of justice, reconciled mankind to the Father, and attained the redemptive power required to cleanse human souls of their earth stains.

When I was a young man, still in high school, I became interested in the scriptures and doctrines relating to the Redemption. I studied the subject of the Atonement many times over a period of years, and came to have what I thought was a good understanding of the doctrines of the Fall, the Atonement, and the plan of salvation. But in retrospect, it is clear that my understanding was largely intellectual in nature. Those doctrines remained formal and abstract explanations to me until I came to receive a personal witness of the living reality and surpassing love of Jesus Christ. I came to appreciate that he had suffered intensely for my sins, that he was a living, personal Savior, and that he had borne my sins because of a love beyond compare. It was then, for the first time in my life, that my heart virtually broke as I thought of what he endured, and love and tears for him overflowed as I realized what he had done for me. President David O. McKay once wrote a letter to his son in which he suggested that the power of Christ's love for us—and the reciprocal love we come to have for him—is the real power of the Atonement in our daily lives. When we truly love him, we want to serve him and do his will. All the doubts and "whys" vanish away.

I have found this to be true in my own life. The testimony I have of the reality and love of Jesus Christ has been the compass of my life. I received that testimony as a young man, eighteen years of age. It was no abstract testimony nor intellectual experience. It was a pure, burning witness of the Spirit that he lives, that he is my Redeemer and Friend in every time of need. Before receiving that witness, my loyalty to the Church was based largely on a sense of duty and a commitment to obey gospel principles and laws. The witness of the Holy Ghost that Christ was a real, living being who knew me and cared about me, transformed my commitment—indeed, my whole life—to a higher plane. I no longer viewed the gospel simply as a set of principles and laws. *My loyalty was to a living being.* I came to understand that I must not trust in my own strength, but instead rely "wholly upon the merits of him who is mighty to save" (2 Nephi 31:19). Soaring hope and "the peace of God, which passeth all understanding" (Philippians 4:7) were the consequent fruits.

With this testimony, let me return to the meaning of Easter, for now at last we are united together as a family in celebration of the resurrection of our Lord. Easter is a celebration of life, of new beginnings and reborn hope. It is the springtime feast. The word *Easter* derives from the medieval Anglo-Saxon goddess of spring—*Eostre or Ostera*—and was originally connected with a Norse celebration of the spring equinox and the budding forth of new flowers. Christianity converted the festival into a memoriam of Christ's resurrection. It is appropriate that springtime and the resurrection be linked, for Christ arose on a spring day, and his resurrection symbolized the birth of new life for all mankind.

And yet Easter means so much more than physical resurrection. For me, Easter symbolizes the total and consummate triumph of our Lord over death, evil, and a fallen world. That brilliant Easter morning is an everlasting reminder that while there is opposition in all things, life and light and truth and God will ultimately prevail. The resurrection is proof that our universe is fundamentally good and benevolent—the right really does always triumph over the wrong in the end. I marvel to think that the resurrection took place only about thirty-six hours or so after Christ's searing cry of anguish on the cross. We speak of three days, but the interval by the Jewish calendar was only thirty-six hours, from the evening of Passover Friday to the early morning of Sunday next. How swiftly the darkness of the Crucifixion turned to the light of the resurrection morn! To outside observers witnessing Christ's torment and death on the cross, it appeared that the world had defeated him. But to the contrary, he had overcome the world, becoming its master and king in the highest meaning possible.

His was a victory heralded by uncounted hosts in the spirit world. At Golgotha, in the last moments of this mortal life, the Savior bowed his head and declared, "Father, into thy hands I commend my spirit" (Luke 23:46), and he voluntarily relinquished his body to death. From one instant to the next, he entered the spirit world, where a remarkable assembly of the deceased awaited him. Joseph F. Smith, the sixth President of the Church, saw in vision the glorious assemblage gathered in anticipation of his advent into the spirit world: "While this vast multitude waited and conversed, rejoicing in the hour of their deliverance from the chains of death, the Son of God appeared, declaring liberty to the captives who had been faithful. . . . And the saints rejoiced in their redemption, and bowed the knee and acknowledged the Son of God as their Redeemer and Deliverer from death and the chains of hell. Their countenances shone, and the radiance from the presence of the Lord rested upon them, and they sang praises unto his holy name" (D&C 138:18, 23–24).

This marvelous scene was followed by Jesus organizing the work of redemption and the preaching of the gospel in the spirit world, thus extending the full blessings of the Atonement to all who had lived before his mortal life. While darkness and gloom reigned in Jerusalem, joy and gladness resounded among the hosts of the dead.

Then came Easter morning. I picture it as a bright springtime day in the Holy City. The Mediterranean sun that shines on Jerusalem's mountain plateau diffuses through desert dust, forming a unique, golden light even today. I am certain it shone with exceptional radiance that April morning. Commissioned of the Father and possessing a fulness of divine power and authority, the Son of God consummated his victory over death and reclaimed possession of his physical body, restoring it not only to life, but to a higher state of celestial glory and perfection. The bands that bound his body were broken, the stone that blocked the grave rolled aside, and the Redeemer came forth in brilliant triumph, the firstfruits of a resurrection that would eventually encompass the entire human race. Jesus' agony was over. Love's redeeming work was done. He had opened heaven's gate!

The resurrection occurred in a garden not far from Golgotha. Thus, Christ's victory over death and his triumph over sin at Gethsemane both took place in garden settings. How fitting and right, for "the earth was once a garden place," and in the end of time, it will be a resplendent garden once again, a millennial Eden made possible by Christ's high conquests in two obscure Jerusalem gardens long ago. Gardens are places where new life begins and grows. Each spring, the gardens of the world yield up a kind of resurrection, as dormant seeds break forth in new life once again. Easter is our garden holiday, a celebration of springtimes, both temporal and celestial.

So children, this Easter Sunday let us vow in our hearts to dress and make lovely the garden of our lives. Let us follow him, our Master and Lord, in every point. Let us study his word, obey his laws, and yield our hearts to his will. Let us be faithful and true, trusting in him through every trial of life, including the passage known as death, which is really only a new birth. Then at length the time shall come when our spirits will reunite with our bodies in the springtime of the resurrection. In the midst of gardens of unimaginable splendor, heavenly parents and loved ones long departed shall greet us in a reunion without end. In reverence we will bow before our faithful Redeemer, the King of Kings—he who was the firstfruits of the resurrection, he who ascended to the Father that first Easter morning with exultant angels as his escort and healing in his wings. All glory be his!

With love,
Your father

CHAPTER TWO
UNTO US A CHILD IS BORN

In twelfth century Europe, the Catholic friars who labored in the monasteries of the day sang a particular Gregorian chant to commemorate the birth of Jesus. They would sing it each evening during the week preceding Christmas, at Vespers, both before and after the recitation of the Magnificat. The first verse of this medieval carol is well known today; the other verses less so. Each stanza calls upon the Savior to come to earth, each petitioning him by a different name:

> *O come, o come, Immanuel,*
> *And ransom captive Israel;*
> *That mourns in lowly exile here,*
> *Until the Son of God appear;*
>
> *O come, O come, Thou Rod of Jesse, free*
> *Thine own from Satan's tyranny;*
> *From depths of hell Thy people save*
> *And give them victory o'er the grave.*
>
> *O come, Thou Dayspring, come and cheer*
> *Our spirit by Thine advent here;*
> *Disperse the gloomy clouds of night,*
> *And death's dark shadows put to flight.*

O come, Thou Key of David, come
And open wide our heavenly home;
Make safe the way that leads on high
And close the path to misery.

O come, O come, Thou Lord of might,
Who once from Sinai's flaming height
Didst give the trembling tribes Thy law,
In glory, majesty, and awe.

Rejoice, rejoice, Immanuel shall come to thee,
  O Israel.[1]

He came in the quiet of the night, in the meridian of time, he who was Immanuel, the Rod of Jesse, the Dayspring, the Key of David, the very Lord of Might. His birth marked the promised visitation of the Creator to earth, the condescension of God to man. As Isaiah wrote of the event, "The people that walked in darkness have seen a great light: they that dwell in the land of the shadow of death, upon them hath the light shined" (Isaiah 9:2).

We know from modern revelation that Jesus Christ was born on April 6, making it early springtime in Judaea when the anointed King of Israel came to earth. As Micah had prophesied, he was born in Bethlehem, "little among the thousands of Judah" (Micah 5:2). The village of his birth lay in the shadow of mighty Jerusalem, six miles to the northeast. Jerusalem was the capital city of Judaea, seat of the temple, and bastion of Roman power. Bethlehem-Ephratah, by contrast, was a pastoral town, homespun and agrarian in all its ways. Its one claim to renown was as the birthplace of David, ancient king of Israel; hence, its common designation as "the City of

David." Its Hebrew name, *Bet Lehem*, meant "House of Bread," an appellation that was of no particular significance until he was born who would be known as the Bread of Life.

The fields surrounding Bethlehem were home to numerous flocks of sheep, and the month of April was a traditional birthing season for the ewes of the flock, with lambs born almost every night. In their awkward role of midwives to the animals, the shepherds would have stayed up most of the night, laboring beneath the crystal sky of the desert plateau; hence, the angels who heralded his birth would not have needed to wake them.

The boy child who arrived that birthing season was known as "the Lamb of God." It is a title of deep significance, for he arrived with the lambs and would someday be "brought as a lamb to the slaughter" (Isaiah 53:7). Yet paradoxically, he was also the Good Shepherd, one who cares for the lambs. Thus, in a curious way, the twin symbols of his life would represent both those who serve and those who are served. It was only right that Christ should play both roles, for in life he "descended below all things" (D&C 88:6), and in eternity he "ascended on high" and is in and through and "round about all things" (D&C 88:6, 41). He knew life from every side and every angle, both above and below. He was the greatest, who made himself least; the heavenly Shepherd who became a lamb.

His coming was more than simply the birth of a great prophet or religious leader, the advent of a promised heir to the royal throne, or even the arrival of the greatest being who would ever walk the earth. It was all of that, of course, but it was something far greater—the coming of the God of heaven to "walk upon his footstool and be like man almost."[2] In the words of a famous carol, "He came down to earth from heaven, Who is God and Lord of all."[3] Jesus Christ was the Creator who spoke with Adam in the beginning and who revealed himself to all the holy prophets from Adam down to the day of his Nativity. It was his voice that resounded on Mount Sinai; his power that upheld chosen Israel in its wanderings; his presence revealed to the brother of Jared, to Moses, and to a select few prophets who witnessed his countenance while they were still in the flesh. And therein lies the greatest miracle of the Nativity: when the Great Jehovah, God and Creator of heaven and earth, first revealed himself in person to the world at large, he chose to do so in the form of an infant, helpless and dependent, born in the same manner as any human being was ever born.

His divinity set him apart from other mortals, notwithstanding that he would share their tribulations in the fullest degree. He was the literal son of the Highest—the Only Begotten of the Father in the flesh. Though Joseph and Mary would be known to family and neighbors as his parents, only Mary in truth was his literal mother. Joseph was in actuality his step-father, a loving and good one, no doubt. His literal father was Elohim—God the Father, the Man of Holiness, Supreme Being of the universe. Christ's physical body inherited the seeds of mortality from his mother and the seeds of immortality from his Father. This imparted a dual nature to his being—part human and mortal; part divine and immortal. Son of God and Son of Woman. This was in accordance with the plan of redemption from the beginning: Christ's divine nature would give him the necessary measure of strength to endure the insurmountable burdens he would bear, while also making possible the voluntary surrender of his life at Calvary. Ordinary human suffering and wounds could not kill him—he had the power to freely keep or relinquish his life as he chose. Such divinity may seem to have given him an advantage over other mortals, but in fact it meant that Christ could and would suffer far more than any other human, without succumbing to the relief of unconsciousness or physical demise. As King Benjamin prophesied, he would suffer "even more than man can suffer, except it be unto death" (Mosiah 3:7).

Students of the Bible have reason to believe that the shepherds to whom the angels appeared were the keepers of the temple flocks, a conjecture based on an ancient Jewish tradition that the Messiah would be revealed from *Migdal Eder,* "the tower of the flock." The Jewish interpretive text of the *Mishnah* suggests that this could mean none other than the special flocks consecrated to the temple.[4] If this is so, then lambs born years later into those same flocks may have been among those offered in the temple at the time of Christ's Passover sacrifice on the cross. Whether this is so or not, it is certainly the case that his atoning sacrifice was portended even in his birth. An ancient Hebrew tradition held that the Messiah would be born on the Passover. And from astronomical calculation we know that April 6 in the meridian of time was indeed the day of the Passover Feast, that sacred Jewish commemoration of Israel's salvation from the destroying angel that meant death for the firstborn sons of Egypt. It was a salvation granted to each Israelite family that sacrificed a lamb and smeared its blood on the wooden doorposts of their dwelling. Thirty-three years

23

after his Passover birth, Christ's blood would be smeared on the wooden posts of a cross to save his people from the destroying angels of death and sin.

Since April 6 was the high day of the Passover Feast, that celebration may have been the reason why there was no room at the inn—the population of Jerusalem swelled by tens of thousands during Passover, forcing travelers to seek accommodations in outlying towns. Mary and Joseph went to Bethlehem, the home of Joseph's forefathers, in order to fulfill the requirements of the imperial census ordered by Caesar Augustus—what Luke calls "this taxing," since it was held for the purpose of determining tax rates. The requirement of the census allowed them to make their appearance in Bethlehem at any time during the year, but they very likely chose the Passover season, because it was a requirement of the Mosaic law for all males to present themselves in Jerusalem at this time (the attendance of women was optional, but customary).[5] Because Bethlehem was virtually next door to the Holy City, the couple from Nazareth could take care of two obligations at once.

The innkeeper has come down in history with somewhat of a notorious reputation. Yet given the crowding that took place throughout the region of Jerusalem at Passover, we can hardly blame him for having no room to offer the couple from Nazareth. While the majority of Passover pilgrims would spend their visit in thousands of goatskin tents pitched on the plains around Jerusalem, many others would seek refuge in the local caravansaries or *khans* as they were known, filling them to capacity. The inn in Bethlehem no doubt was overflowing, and the innkeeper's offering of the stable was very likely an act of genuine kindness, for it was the custom of the Judaeans to offer strangers and pilgrims sojourn in their homes whenever possible.

Even had the couple found room in the inn, it would have offered only primitive accommodations: a typical *khan* of the period was a stone structure consisting of a series of bare-walled rooms, each with only three walls and open to public view on one side. Crowded and noisy, the rooms were devoid of furniture, and the *khan* provided no services. The stable itself was likely a walled courtyard or even a limestone cave, where animals belonging to the guests or the innkeeper were kept.[6] It would have been a place of filth and foul odors, though offering some refuge from wind and cold. Whether courtyard, cave, or other refuge, Christ's birth among the animals did have one conspicuous advantage over the crowded interior of the *khan*—here at least was to be found peace and privacy. In this sense, the offering of the stable was a blessing, allowing the most sacred birth in human history to take place in quiet solitude, hidden from the eyes of men.

We recognize the lowly stable as part of the condescension of God, of Christ's willingness to submit to all things as he traversed earth life. But there is more to it than this. Our Father in Heaven, in whose hands all power lies, could have arranged for his Only Begotten to be born anyplace, at any time, and in any circumstances. If he had wanted Christ to be born in a palace, surrounded by wealth and earthly pageantry, it would have been done. That he was born instead in a lowly village, in an obscure stable, to a peasant woman of no fame or standing, was no accident, but an integral part of the divine plan, a message of truth from God to us.

His birth, like his life, teaches us that there is nothing wrong with humble origins, with poverty, simplicity, and obscurity. There is nothing to be ashamed of in being outcast from society, in being forced to dwell apart from the world, literally or figuratively. Poverty is no disgrace, and a shelter for animals may be a temple of the Lord's spirit as surely as any more elegant dwelling. It does not matter how the world measures worth; if God and his servants pay respect—as did the shepherds, the angels, and later the wise men—then the opinions of the world are dross and straw. Christ's birth and simple upbringing are a reminder to us that we must never look down on anyone because of their origins or worldly status. If we scorn the humble, we may unwittingly scorn the chosen of God's children on the earth.

The Nativity is replete with other evidences of God's love for the humble. The heavenly hosts who proclaimed Christ's birth in song appeared not to the Sanhedrin, not to the Herodian court, not even to the priests carrying out their Passover duties in the temple. They appeared to lowly shepherds abiding with their flocks by night. Perhaps nowhere in Judaea were there more humble and simple souls than these shepherds, and none would have received the gladsome tidings more readily than they who "came with haste," glorifying and praising God. Likewise, Simeon and Anna, who came to the temple as guided by the Spirit and beheld the newborn child on the eighth day of his mortality, were among the most plain of Israel. Both were of exceedingly advanced age; yet fired by the inspiration of the Holy Ghost, they came to see the Messiah. The surrounding masses of Judaea, meanwhile, were oblivious to the presence of the Son of God in their midst. Anna and Simeon had waited decades to see his face before they died; the latter's prayer of rejoicing on that day is recorded forever as holy writ in the Book of Luke, the sublime poetry known in Christian tradition as the *Nunc Dimittis* (Luke 2:29–32). As it is written, "God resisteth the proud, but giveth grace unto the humble" (James 4:6).

There were at least two other groups of people who received heavenly tidings of his advent: the "wise men from the east" spoken of by Matthew, and the Nephite population in the New World, astonished by the fulfillment of Samuel the Lamanite's prophecy that at Christ's birth a day and a night would pass without darkness. With respect to the wise men, the Bible Dictionary, under the heading "Magi," says, "It seems likely that they were representatives of a branch of the Lord's people somewhere from east of Palestine, who had come, led by the Spirit, to behold the Son of God, and who returned to their people to bear witness that the King Immanuel had indeed been born in the flesh." If they were emissaries from a remnant of Israel, we may someday read an account of their journey in scripture yet promised to come forth (2 Nephi 29:12–13), just as the Nephites learned of his birth from their own prophets and made a scriptural record of the same. The exceptional treatment afforded the scattered remnants of Israel at the time of his birth (and later, at his death) remind us that while Christ is the Savior of the whole earth, his mortal ministry was specifically centered on the House of Israel, whose literal King by right of lineage he was.

Herod, ruler of Palestine under Rome, also received tidings of Christ's birth, albeit not from heavenly messengers, but secondhand from the Magi. Surrounded by decadence and the impregnable might of the Roman legions, his soul was mired in misery, having personally ordered numerous acts of mass murder, including the assassination of several close family members. Herod's reaction to the news of Christ's birth was archetypal of the reaction of worldly power everywhere to tidings of righteousness' advance: he felt threatened. Though nearing the end of his days and as secure on his throne as any tyrant could possibly be, he panicked at word that a peasant child had been born whose right to reign might surpass in legitimacy his own. Feigning a desire to worship the child, he sent armed troops to slaughter the infants of Bethlehem, adding one more diadem of evil to a life steeped in wickedness. It is ironic that Herod's palace fortress lay but a few miles from Bethlehem on the hill known today as *Jebel Fureidês* or "Little Paradise Mountain." Looming dark against the night, it would have dominated the horizon as Joseph and Mary made their way past Jerusalem to Bethlehem; and no doubt its frightening visage confronted them again when they fled from Herod's wrath to Egypt. The forces that would stalk and persecute the Savior throughout his life were not far removed even in his birth.

Luke observes that baby Jesus was wrapped in swaddling clothes and laid in a manger (Luke 2:7). Here too lie divine portents. That Christ was wrapped in swaddling clothes, his arms bound tightly to his body, may be seen as a symbol of his submission to the constraints and limitations of mortal life; it reminds us that he was as helpless and dependent in birth as any child ever born. Though legends abound as to the magical powers of the infant Christ, none of these appear in scripture, and we have no reason to accept them. When the Lord came down to earth, he truly came *down*. Like any infant, he would have forgotten all—the glory of his premortal past lay behind the veil, and he would learn and grow "line upon line" like any child.

That the Savior's first bed was a manger seems also a token from on high. A manger is a trough from which animals feed. Though only a baby, he was destined to become the Bread of Life, the one true source of spiritual nourishment for all mankind. He would later declare: "I am the living bread which came down from heaven: if any man eat of this bread, he shall live for ever: and the bread that I will give is my flesh, which I will give for the life of the world. . . . Except ye eat the flesh of the Son of man, and drink his blood, ye have no life in you" (John 6:51, 53). Christ's declaration was spiritual, not literal, in meaning; but the same sacramental message was prefigured in the Nativity, as he slept in a feeding trough.

The humble circumstances of Christ's birth do not in the least degree detract from his divinity or diminish his royalty. In the words of Sir Matthew Hale, "Thy presence, Lord, alone; will make a stall a court, a cratch a throne."[7] No manger can alter the fact that he was the legitimate, rightful heir to the throne of Israel. By lineage and birthright, he was literally the King of the Jews. In the centuries since the division of the kingdom upon Solomon's death, the true royal lineage had become corrupted and usurped beyond recognition by political intrigue and Roman conquest. Hence, no one knew who was the rightful heir to the throne of David, though Herod's own claim was patently bogus, the whole Herodian line being little more than lackeys of Roman power. It was the illegitimacy of Herod's rule that caused him to tremble and order the slaughter of the innocents after the wise men brought word of a child whose right it was to reign.

Certainly in the ensuing years none suspected that the legitimate line of succession might pass through humble Nazareth, where Mary and Joseph dwelled. But so it was, and the Gospel writers take pains to review Christ's lineage in detail, making the case that he was indeed the rightful heir to the throne of Israel. Thus, he was king not only by heavenly appointment, but also by right of earthly law—a direct descendant of David, through whose lineage it was prophesied that Messiah would come: "Of the increase of his government and peace there shall be no end, upon the throne of David, and upon his kingdom, to order it, and to establish it with judgment and with justice from henceforth even for ever" (Isaiah 9:7). Jesus Christ was the Second David, anointed by God to gather, unite, and redeem the House of Israel spiritually, even as David had established it as a united kingdom temporally.[8] How right, then, that he should be born in the City of David, birthplace of Jesse's son and the village where the prophet Samuel had anointed the shepherd boy as the future king of Israel, inaugurating the Davidic dynasty on earth.

The infant King came to a people plunged in darkness, a broken remnant of the once exalted House of Israel. Fallen from their days of glory under David and Solomon, the Israelites of Palestine were lineal descendants of but one and a half of the original twelve tribes, the other ten and a half tribes having been carried into Assyrian exile and lost to history more than seven hundred years before his coming. Reduced in numbers and sunk in apostasy, Israel chafed under despotic vassals appointed by Rome. Even the holy temple at Jerusalem had been built with Roman funds by the tyrant Herod. At the time Jesus lived, the sacred edifice lay under the control of a hypocritical generation of religious leaders; it was daily desecrated by money-changers and merchants, who trafficked dishonestly in the tokens of divine sacrifice.

Benighted Israel desperately needed him who was their Messiah, yet "He came unto his own, and his own received him not" (John 1:11). Israel's expectation of a Messiah was that of an all-powerful political leader who would free Palestine from Roman rule and restore its imperial grandeur for all time. The chosen people were simply unprepared for a Messiah who came as a carpenter from Nazareth, preaching the gospel of peace and seeking to free Israel from the bondage of sin, instead of from Rome. Ironically, had they received him who was their Lord and God, the resultant spiritual renewal would have paved the way for political freedom, averting the catastrophic destruction of Jerusalem and the temple in 70 A.D. But so happy an ending was not to be. Though a star heralded his birth, the only official recognition of his kingship would be the declaration that heathen Pilate nailed above his cross.

The chroniclers of the New Testament trace the royal birthright of the Messiah through Joseph, probably because the temporal rights of kingship were always passed down through male lines. But we know that Mary, too, was a descendant of David; hence, Christ's right to the throne of Israel was established in both lineages. The Book of Mormon describes Mary as "a virgin, most beautiful and fair above all other virgins" (1 Nephi 11:15). She was the chosen vessel of God for the delivery of his son to earth, a handmaiden "highly favoured" and "blessed . . . among women" (Luke 1:28). There are many women of great faith and virtue in the scriptures, but as Bruce R. McConkie observed, there was only one Mary and none quite like her.[9] Upon entering Mary's presence, her cousin Elizabeth felt her own child—the future John the Baptist—leap within her womb, and filled with the spirit of prophecy, she declared, "And whence is this to me, that the mother of my Lord should come to me?" (Luke 1:43). Though Latter-day Saints do not worship Mary, as some Christian denominations do, she was an elect woman, whose life and mission merit our highest respect and admiration. Her place in the first Advent setting is never to be forgotten, a sacred image reproduced thousands of times over in artistic expression through the ages: Mary serene with divine light, holding to her bosom the infant king, "the hopes and fears of all the years" met in one that night.

Mary's experience in giving birth to Jesus becomes all the more poignant when we consider how weary she must have been after the eighty-mile journey from Nazareth to Bethlehem, a journey made more arduous by her advanced pregnancy. Then after the journey came the long and frustrating search for shelter, probably for hours on end. And when at last a refuge of a sort was found, she soon began the pangs of childbirth, notwithstanding her weakened condition. Every mother sacrifices by the suffering entailed in childbirth, and Mary was no exception. Yet she had the comfort of knowing that her newborn child was the Anointed of God, the promised Messiah of the ages, and the solace of that knowledge must have transcended all travail. The visitation of the shepherds, who came telling of heavenly choirs and angelic pronouncements, no doubt confirmed her joy in that assurance. What thoughts filled her mind we can only guess. The scriptures say simply that "Mary kept all these things, and pondered them in her heart" (Luke 2:19). The time would come, as Simeon prophesied, that a sword would pierce through her own soul also, a day when she would be forced to witness her son's agony on the cross. But for the moment, on this one day of days, peace reigned. The Creator, veiled in flesh, had come to walk the earth.

THE SPIRIT OF CHRISTMAS PRESENT

Six days before Christmas 1843, Charles Dickens published *A Christmas Carol*, a work destined to rank among the most beloved tales of all time. It is an account of one Ebenezer Scrooge, an old miser who learns hard lessons about life, happiness, and Christmas, as taught to him by the spirits of Christmas past, present, and future. In the end, after an awful vision of the darkness of his own soul, Scrooge begs for, and is given, a second chance. Filled with the spirit of Christmas, he turns his life around and becomes "as good a friend, as good a master, and as good a man, as the good old city knew, or any other good old city, town, or borough, in the good old world."[10] Dickens's work is as much about repentance as about Christmas. Unfortunately, the name "Scrooge" even today is applied to anyone who scorns the spirit of Christmas, but it should not rightly be so, for as Dickens wrote of Scrooge after his transformation, "he knew how to keep Christmas well, if any man alive possessed the knowledge."[11]

It falls to each of us, like Ebenezer, to find the true meaning of Christmas and learn "how to keep Christmas well." I have heard the opinion expressed that Christmas is for children. Certainly the special magic of the season stems in part from childhood, when family traditions weave lifelong memories and gift-giving elicits a warm glow of anticipation. But age and maturity will not diminish the spirit of Christmas if we learn, as Christ admonished, to "receive the kingdom of God as a little child" (Mark 10:15). As Charles Dickens observed in a A Christmas Carol, "It is good to be children sometimes, and never better than at Christmas, when its mighty Founder was a child himself."[12]

For both children and adults, the true spirit of Christmas will always be linked to the birth of Jesus Christ and to love of the Savior. Children who receive gifts at Christmas without understanding the meaning of the day will not cherish their Yuletide experience quite so dearly, no matter how lavish the spending and celebration may be. Children receive gifts at birthday parties too, but the spirit of such occasions does not approach that of Christmas. Traditions and gifts have their place, but not center place. Christmas as it ought to be will ever mean Christmas centered on the Savior and his birth.

As we invite the light of Christ into our lives, the whole season becomes a sacramental commemoration of his birth—and not of his birth alone, but of his life, his resurrection, and his Eternal Lordship. As President Gordon B. Hinckley has said: "The story of Christmas is so much larger than the story of His birth in Bethlehem . . . His birth cannot be separated from His earthly ministry. Neither can it be detached from His divine sacrifice, the atonement made in behalf of each of us. At Christmas, we sing of His birth. I feel so profoundly grateful for that birth. But that birth would not be remembered but for the gift He made to all of us through His mortal ministry, followed by the terrible pain and suffering of His death, to rise glorious and triumphant as the Redeemer of the world."[13]

A sacred feeling fills the air during the Christmas season, almost like a premonition of heavenly hosts rejoicing high above the earth. A spirit of peace moves across the earth, touching even the unbelieving and the heathen. There have been wars in which cease-fires were declared at Christmas, with enemy combatants fraternizing on that one day alone. It is a season when statesmen still their machinations, families draw together, and the world partakes of a celebration of memory and brotherhood. What accounts for the unique spirit of the season? I believe the spirit of God sheds forth more abundantly whenever men's hearts are turned from selfish thoughts to thoughts of family, friends, and God. This Yuletide outpouring of the spirit is a tribute to the Redeemer's mission, and though the exalted spirit of Christmas may dwindle in the face of materialism or indifference, its presence is undeniable to all who understand the significance of his birth.

Perhaps the most cherished Christmas of my life was one in which no gifts were given, no traditions kept, and no family nearby. I was a missionary in the Germany Düsseldorf Mission, and the year was 1972. My companion and I were assistants to the mission president, and that Christmas day, nearly twenty baptisms were scheduled to take place across the mission—a record number for one day. Our responsibility was to travel to as many of these baptismal services as possible, representing the mission president. We rose early on Christmas Day and departed for the northern cities of the mission, nearly five hours away. Never had I spent a Christmas so austere as this, yet light seemed to fill the air, and our hearts rejoiced. This was the work of God; this was why Christ came to earth; this labor was the highest tribute we could possibly pay to him on this day. In the city of Minden, a family of seven was baptized, and the whole branch turned out for the occasion, feeling as we did that there was no better way to celebrate Christmas than this. We then drove to another city and baptism, then finally returned to Düsseldorf for a baptism scheduled late in the evening. The whole day was nothing but travel and baptisms, yet never before in my life had I felt the spirit of Christmas more deeply. We were witnessing the giving of a gift that would last forever. The Savior's spirit was near that day, which I will ever regard as embodying the highest meaning of Christmas.

As I learned that day, Christmas is still Christmas even without any of its traditions or worldly accoutrements; neither material gifts nor traditions are its essence, and their absence cannot detract from the true spirit of the day. This does not mean that traditions can play no part in our keeping Christmas well. Intermingled with the sacred, traditions can be more than rituals of remembrance; they can embody the highest meaning of Christmas. If we were to look at our Christmas traditions with spiritual eyes, we might better understand Christ's declaration that "all things bear record of me" (Moses 6:63).

Consider, for example, the Christmas tree. In origin, it is said to stem from a heathen celebration connected with the winter solstice, the shortest day of the year. (Heathen reverence for the winter solstice apparently was the reason the

Romans moved the celebration of Christ's birth to late December.) As such, the Christmas tree may appear as a very un-Christian graft onto a Christian holiday. Yet it need not be seen as such, for the tree presents a beautiful symbol of the Savior himself. It is an evergreen, a token of life everlasting, even in the dark of winter and storm. While the evergreen tree is the most simple and natural of creations, it is at the same time stately and majestic, reminding us that he who was "a root out of a dry ground" (Isaiah 53:2) was the very personification of manliness and royal majesty.

The Christmas tree also brings to mind Nephi's famous vision of the tree of life, for when Nephi sought an interpretation as to the significance of the tree which he saw, his angel courier showed him a vision of Mary and the birth of Jesus:

"And I looked and beheld the virgin again, bearing a child in her arms.

"And the angel said unto me: Behold the Lamb of God, yea, even the Son of the Eternal Father! *Knowest thou the meaning of the tree which thy father saw?*

"*And I answered him, saying: Yea, it is the love of God, which sheddeth itself abroad in the hearts of the children of men; wherefore, it is the most desirable above all things.*

"And he spake unto me, saying: Yea, and the most joyous to the soul" (1 Nephi 11:20–23; emphasis added).

The tree of life is the love of God, and an angel of God seeking to capture the power of that love could find no higher expression than the birth of the Son of God. When I admire our Christmas tree each year, I think of this vision and remember that Christ himself is as the tree of life, the very embodiment of God's love toward his children.

Other Christmas traditions, regardless of their secular origins, may also contain hidden symbolism of divine truths. Elder Neal A. Maxwell, speaking at the lighting of the Christmas lights at Temple Square in 1997, drew an analogy between the myriads of tiny lights and the galaxies above: "Our solar system within the Milky Way Galaxy has only one sun, and yet our sun is only one of millions of like stars in our Milky Way Galaxy. Thus, if each and every one of the three-quarters of a million tiny, little lights just about to be turned on, represented an entire and huge galaxy, it would still be far, far short of God's vast and stunning creations."[14] Elder Maxwell also likened the lights to the membership of the Church: "There are now more than 10 million members of the Church. If each of us were truly a light, how much more warm and lighted the world would be."[15]

In similar fashion, we can find divine tokens of truth in many of our Christmas traditions, transforming them from mere customs into reminders of Christ's lordship. The candy cane is widely recognized as a reproduction of a shepherd's staff. The Christmas wreath originated in remembrance of the crown of thorns worn by the Savior on the cross; it may also remind us that God's plan is "one eternal round." Similarly, Christmas bells can serve as heralds of his coming, while Christmas candles symbolize the light of the world that shines in the darkness (John 1:4–5). Even the Christmas stockings hung by the fireplace may bring to mind those who have neither shoes nor stockings, whose store of worldly goods is bare, prompting us to reach out and share with the needy at this time of year. In the symbols and traditions of Christmas, all things bear record of him.

The most common Christmas tradition of all is the giving of gifts, a tradition begun by the Magi when they brought their offerings of gold, frankincense, and myrrh. How appropriate to commemorate the Savior's birth by giving, since he gave the ultimate gift to all mankind. Unfortunately, the commercialism of modern society has robbed this tradition of some of its value, turning what ought to be a selfless ritual of sharing into a sometimes crass and materialistic habit. But it need not be so. If our hearts are centered on Christ, we need not fall prey to the superficialities of commercialism. Perhaps giving gifts would hold greater meaning if we gave less of what can be purchased in stores and more of what we alone can give. Likewise, if we would agree to give less to each other and more to the poor and needy, we would rediscover the magic of Christmas one hundred fold.

One final thought about gift-giving. Though the King Immanuel does not need our material goods, it is still possible to give a gift to him whose birthday it is. In the sentiment of Christina Rossetti:

> *What can I give Him,*
> *Poor as I am?*
> *If I were a shepherd,*
> *I would bring a lamb,*
> *If I were a Wise Man,*
> *I would do my part,—*
> *Yet what can I give Him?*
> *Give my heart.*[16]

A pure heart, willing and broken, is the offering we can give him all year long. As Creator of the world and all things therein, there is really little else—and nothing higher—we can offer him.

The Christmas season ought to be a time to remember those for whom there is still no room in the inn—the lonely and outcast. In the city of Nauvoo on Christmas 1843, an incident took place that personified the truth that God includes all in his grace; none are ever excluded who humbly seek him. We know of it from the journal of the prophet Joseph Smith. A grand Christmas celebration was taking place in the Nauvoo Mansion, to which all the great citizens of the city had been invited, along with many important visitors and guests. The prophet writes:

> A large party supped at my house, and spent the evening in music, dancing, &c., in a most cheerful and friendly manner. During the festivities, a man with his hair long and falling over his shoulders, and apparently drunk, came in and acted like a Missourian. I requested the captain of the police to put him out of doors. A scuffle ensued, and I had an opportunity to look him full in the face, when, to my great surprise and joy untold, I discovered it was my long-tried, warm, but cruelly persecuted friend, Orrin Porter Rockwell, just arrived from nearly a year's imprisonment, without conviction, in Missouri.[17]

Porter Rockwell was a rugged mountain man with little regard for the finer things of life, a man whose manners and dress might easily have offended the more refined among the Saints. Yet the Prophet, seeing beneath the rough exterior a heart of gold, welcomed him to the Christmas celebration with "joy untold." Had not Christ also dined with unwashed commoners and publicans, even counting one of the latter among his apostles? That Nauvoo celebration was to be the last Christmas Day in the life of the Prophet Joseph Smith.

A TIME FORETOLD

The birth of Immanuel marked the first coming of the Messiah to his people, but not the last. A time is coming when a new heaven and earth shall own the Prince of Peace their king. At that day, Jesus Christ will come not in a lowly stable nor an obscure village, but as a Bright and Morning Star from the east, "glorious in his apparel, travelling in the greatness of his strength" (Isaiah 63:1). With power and might he shall assume his rightful place as David's heir, and in righteousness he shall rule the world for a thousand years. "No more will sin and sorrow grow, nor thorns infest the ground; He'll come and make the blessings flow far as the curse was found."[18]

The advent of Christ's millennial reign will fulfill the angelic anthem sung above the plains of Palestine on the night of his birth: in literal reality, glory shall be to God in the highest, and on earth, peace and good will shall reign among men. Graced by the presence of its Creator, Earth will become Eden, and every nation, kindred, tongue, and people be blessed. A sound of jubilation shall ring out, as the righteous remnant of God's children extol the coronation of Immanuel as King of Kings—and the whole world sends back the song which then the angels sang.

CHAPTER THREE

THE PRINCE AND THE PRODIGALS

The most famous parable of the Savior, and perhaps his most poignant, is the parable of the prodigal son (Luke 15:11–32). It is a story calculated to touch our innermost feelings. We all know of sons or daughters who have strayed from home, and every parent sympathizes with the heartache of the father who loves his son despite the latter's delinquency. Few classics of literature can equal the emotion kindled by the reconciliation between father and son that takes place at the end of the parable.

Yet for all its pathos, the parable profits from a second, more thoughtful reading. We are accustomed to thinking of the prodigal son as a benighted sinner, foolish and fallen; it may be disconcerting to realize that the Savior had in mind not only grand sinners, but *all* sinners, when he related this tale. The parable of the prodigal son is a parable of us all. It is an allegory of the plan of salvation, teaching the lesson that all of earth's inhabitants are, in some measure, prodigal sons and daughters of their Father in Heaven. As Isaiah said, "All we like sheep have gone astray; we have turned every one to his own way" (Isaiah 53:6). Or in the words of the Apostle Paul,

"All have sinned, and come short of the glory of God" (Romans 3:23).

Like the prodigal son, we dwell in "a far country" (Luke 15:13), a great distance removed from our premortal home. Like him, to the extent that we sin, we squander a portion of our divine inheritance and experience a "mighty famine" of spirit. We learn by painful experience that worldly pleasures are of no more worth than the husks of corn that swine eat, and we, like the prodigal, yearn to return to the peace and security of our Father's home.

In the Savior's parable, only the eldest son remained loyal to his father; in his own words, "neither transgressed I at any time thy commandment" (Luke 15:29). Similarly, in the plan of salvation, the eldest son, or Firstborn of the Father, is sinless and without spot. Yet there is a vital difference. In the Lord's parable, the eldest son is *jealous* of the attention paid to the returning prodigal. In the plan of salvation, however, the eldest son *makes possible* the return of the prodigals. Only through him can the children of God be reconciled with their Father.

In order to understand the significance of this, consider the following allegory of the plan of salvation, "The Parable of the Prince and the Prodigals":

> A certain lord possessed lands, kingdoms, and wealth in abundance. He lived in peace with his sons and daughters, who shared in the riches of his estate and the joy of his love. But it came to pass one day that the children of the great lord grew restless and, desiring to seek estates of their own, came to him and said: "Give us that portion of our inheritance that falls to us, for we would seek our fortune in a distant land."

Not many days hence, the sons and daughters of the great Lord took their journey into a far country, charged with the admonition of their father to preserve their inheritance and not squander it in the world. One child only, the firstborn son, remained at the side of the father. He was prince and heir to the throne.

Many days passed, and the sons and daughters who had gone into the world began to spend their inheritance and waste their substance with riotous living and all manner of foolishness. Soon they had squandered the whole of their fortunes. A mighty famine arose in the land, and the children of the great lord were forced to sell themselves as bond servants to the more prosperous citizens of that country. In time they found themselves herding swine and living in squalor and poverty across the face of the whole land. Nearly perishing for want of food, they ate eagerly even of the husks of corn the swine ate.

When word of their plight reached the great lord, he wept. Then knowing of the devotion of his eldest son, the father sent him forth to redeem his other sons and daughters from bondage. The loyal firstborn vowed to rescue them: "I will save them out of all their dwellingplaces, wherein they have sinned, and will cleanse them" (Ezekiel 37:23).

The prince journeyed the long distance to find and bring the prodigals home. Upon arriving in their land, he found them in appalling conditions: weary, hungry, and downtrodden. He fed them and gave them drink; he lived among them, toiling at their side and sharing their burdens. Then, in a final act of love, the eldest son took of his own fortune and, one by one, he ransomed them. In order to pay the utmost farthing of their debt, he was compelled to sacrifice his entire earthly inheritance, all that he owned, every whit.

Some among the prodigals refused the proffered ransom. Chained by pride, they preferred bondage to contrition. Yet those who forsook their errant ways and accepted of the firstborn's offering received healing at his hands and liberty as his gift. These he led back into the presence of the father with songs of everlasting joy.

After a jubilant homecoming, the prince said, "My father, bring hither the fatted calf, and let us sacrifice it, and make merry, for these thy children were lost and now are found." And with weeping the father embraced him, and said, "My son, in this house shall no more sacrifice be made forevermore, for thine was the supreme offering, which none can equal. Because thou hast done this, thou shalt ever dwell with me, and all that I have is thine."

"Then it is my will," said the son, "To share this gift with these, thy lost ones."

Like the loyal son of this parable, the firstborn son of our Father in Heaven, the Prince of Peace, came to earth to rescue the children of God from their fallen condition. He, the Sinless One, who never transgressed at any time the commandments of the Father, carried our burdens and paid for our sins with his blood. He alone who merited salvation by virtue of his righteousness, turned that righteousness into the currency of our ransom, sacrificing all he had that we might return to our heavenly home. By virtue of his eternal atonement we may receive "all that [the] Father hath" (D&C 84:38).

In the premortal realm, Christ was the God of Abraham, Isaac, and Jacob, the Creator of the Earth, the great I Am.

From these exalted heights, from literal courts on high, he *descended,* coming to earth in the most humble of circumstances that he might become acquainted with our grief. "The King of Kings left worlds of light, became the meek and lowly One."[1] Jesus experienced mortal life in the fullest sense, including all its temptations and suffering, literally walking among us as one of his names—Immanuel or "God with Us"— implies. He might have won political power and honor; he chose instead to be a teacher and healer. He might have earned the favor of his people by freeing them from Roman oppression; instead, he saved them from their sins and was "rejected by his own."[2] In the closing days of his ministry, he sacrificed the peace of Galilee to face humiliation in Jerusalem. There, in the Garden of Gethsemane, the Lord Jesus Christ bore the ultimate weight of the universe as he descended beneath all things. Following a mockery of a trial, he suffered an excruciating death at the hands of men for whose very sins he had atoned. In a most literal way, the Prince of Glory paid the utmost farthing of our ransom, as he bore "the pain of all men" (D&C 18:11). Only the Creator could atone for his creation; only a just and innocent one could offer himself a sacrifice for the guilty.

There are many reasons why Christ descended into our earthly realm of travail. Prominent among them was the necessity that he experience firsthand the trials and temptations of a fallen earth—this that his own compassion might be more perfect, his atoning sacrifice that of one personally familiar with the ordeals of life. The Apostle Paul expressed this in his letter to the Hebrews: "For we have not an high priest which cannot be touched with the feeling of our infirmities; but was in all points tempted like as we are, yet without sin" (Hebrews 4:15).

Alma the Younger in his masterful discourse on the Atonement preached a similar doctrine to the people of Gideon:

"And he shall go forth, suffering pains and afflictions and temptations of every kind; and this that the word might be fulfilled which saith he will take upon him the pains and the sicknesses of his people.

"And he will take upon him death, that he may loose the bands of death which bind his people; and *he will take upon him their infirmities, that his bowels may be filled with mercy, according to the flesh, that he may know according to the flesh how to succor his people according to their infirmities.*

"Now the Spirit knoweth all things; nevertheless the Son of God suffereth according to the flesh that he might take upon him the sins of his people, that he might blot out their transgressions according to the power of his deliverance" (Alma 7:11–13; emphasis added).

Through suffering—not just in Gethsemane or on Calvary, but throughout his thirty-three years of life—the Lord Jesus Christ acquired perfect compassion. By being tempted he learned in a most personal way how to succor (or strengthen) the vulnerable in their temptations. Alma makes clear that "the Spirit knoweth all things," which meant that Christ possessed pure empathy and the powers of deliverance even in his premortal life, when he ruled as Jehovah in the heavens, but by coming down and experiencing the rigors of mortality in the flesh, his compassion and Saviorship reached a fullness of perfection.

THE PRINCE WHO
BECAME A PAUPER

In *The Prince and the Pauper*, Mark Twain tells the tale of two boys: Tom Canty, an impoverished London urchin, and Edward Tudor, Prince of Wales and heir to the English throne. The story begins with a comical mix-up that results in the two being confused for one another, with the result that the pauper assumes the place of the prince, and the prince that of the pauper. It happens one day when young Tom wanders near the vicinity of Westminster Palace, hoping to get a glimpse of the prince. When his wish is fulfilled, he is so excited that he presses up against the palace gate, only to be rudely pushed away by the soldiers guarding the palace. Seeing this, Prince Edward is outraged and rebukes his garrison. He invites the young pauper into the palace for a tour and orders him a sumptuous meal. Afterwards, on a whim, the two boys decide to exchange clothing. Prince Edward had always longed to wear less formal clothing, and Tom Canty had often imagined himself as prince. To their surprise, the boys discover in a mirror that the change of clothing has made them look exactly like each other. Indeed, they have "the same eyes, the same voice and manner, the same form and stature, the same face and countenance."[3] The two are virtually twins.

Still dressed in pauper's garb, the prince makes the mistake of leaving the palace, where the soldiers on guard rudely thrust him outside the gates, assuming he is the insolent pauper. His entreaties and indignation earn him only the scorn of the gathered crowd. Inside the palace, meanwhile, the courtiers and attendants of the prince are convinced the prince has gone mad, since Tom Canty keeps insisting he is not the prince. They resolve to cure him and to keep his derangement a secret from all. Against his will, Tom is thrust into the role of a prince and treated with every deference due that office.

Thus begins a sweeping tale that sees Edward Tudor wandering throughout England seeking to be restored to his lawful throne. During his accidental exile, he endures harrowing experiences: he faces beatings and abuse at the hands of Tom Canty's father; he endures the travails of hunger and poverty; he witnesses and shares in the suffering of the common English people; and he sees the terrible cruelty and injustices of England's legal system. By living it himself, Edward learns about the somber reality of the common folk's daily life: he resolves that if he ever regains his rightful place, he will correct many wrongs and make many amends.

In the end, through a remarkable series of events, the mixup is resolved, and Prince Edward is restored to his place in the palace. In the interim he has inherited the royal throne and become King of England. Tom Canty, who plays a key role in his restoration, is rewarded handsomely by the new sovereign. As for King Edward, he reigns henceforth as a just, kind, and compassionate king, much the wiser for having lived as a pauper among his people. And whenever one of his "gilded vassals" is inclined to question the merciful tenor of Edward's rule or his determination to render the laws of England less harsh, the king turns a mournful eye upon him and says, "What dost *thou* know of suffering and oppression? I and my people know, but not thou."[4]

We, too, have a prince who became a pauper. The Lord Jesus Christ came down to earth and lived among the common people of his day in order that he might be a more compassionate, just, and perfect king. He "uncrowned himself to crown us, and put off his robes to put on our rags."[5] Or, as the Apostle Paul said of the Savior, "though he was rich, yet for your sakes he became poor, that ye through his poverty might be rich" (2 Corinthians 8:9). In another epistle, Paul commented: "Wherefore in all things it behoved him to be made like unto his brethren, that he might be a merciful and faithful high priest. . . . For in that he himself hath suffered being tempted, he is able to succour them that are tempted" (Hebrews 2:17–18).

Having walked among us, the Prince of Peace is no stranger to our trials. There is no temptation we face that he has not faced. There is no humiliation, sorrow, or anguish that we will ever know that he has not experienced in greater measure. We may experience ostracism, betrayal, prejudice, or scorn: he faced them daily during his ministry in Palestine. Our lives may seem obscure, our days dull, our talents and accomplishments meager in the eyes of the world: the Lord Christ "made himself of no reputation" (Philippians 2:7) and was as "a root out of a dry ground," having no beauty that we should desire him (Isaiah 53:2). Our friends may abandon us: so did his. The heavens may seem like brass over our heads: Jesus endured the withdrawal of the Spirit in Gethsemane. Having experienced all, he comprehends all. Whatever depths of anguish or misery we may experience, his compassion for our plight is perfect; he knows how to strengthen us in our travail and lead us from it in due time.

The significance of a Savior who experienced in the flesh the trials of this world is distilled in the following poem by Leona B. Gates:

IN HIS STEPS

The road is rough, I said,
*   Dear Lord, there are stones that hurt me so.*
And he said, Dear Child, I understand,
*   I walked it long ago.*

But there is a cool green path, I said
*   Let me walk there for a time.*
No child, He gently answered me,
*   The green road does not climb.*

My burden, I said, is far too great;
*   How can I bear it so?*
My child, said he, I remember its weight.
*   I carried my cross, you know.*

But, I said, I wish there were friends with me
*   Who would make my way their own.*
Ah, yes, he said, Gethsemane
*   Was hard to face alone.*

And so I climbed the stony path,
*   Content at last to know*
That where my Master had not gone
*   I would not need to go.*

And strangely then I found new friends;
The burden grew less sore
As I remembered—long ago
*   He went that way before.*[6]

However rough the road of life may be, we may take comfort in knowing that he has walked the trail before us. We will never tread where he has not gone before.

THE POWER AND SCOPE
OF THE ATONEMENT

Though the Lord Immanuel "walked with us" in enduring the vicissitudes of mortality, it is imperative to understand that his personal suffering far surpassed anything we will ever experience. In the Garden of Gethsemane and again on the cross, he endured not only the physical torture that any mortal might endure; he bore as well the cumulative "pains of every living creature, both men, women, and children, who belong to the family of Adam" (2 Nephi 9:21). As King Benjamin prophesied, Christ would suffer "pain of body, hunger, thirst, and fatigue, *even more than man can suffer,* except it be unto death" (Mosiah 3:7; emphasis added). The immortal seeds in his body—the divine half of his nature—enabled him to experience agony far beyond human endurance without succumbing to death.

Having overcome the world in every point, Christ possesses a redeeming power that is all-embracing and all-encompassing in scope. His light and power permeate every particle and dimension of existence. His Atonement is the foundation of divine mercy, the source of all grace, and the only "means whereby salvation can come unto the children of men" (Mosiah 3:17).

There are many dimensions to the Great Atonement. Most crucial of all, the atoning sacrifice of the Savior covers the immensity of human sin, both individual and collective. Since even the smallest sin opens an impassable gulf between God and man, the sum total of humanity's guilt is beyond comprehension. No mortal could pay that price, but only one who was "infinite and eternal" (Alma 34:10, 14).

The Atonement makes possible the reconciliation of God and sinners; it is the grand mediation between the Father and his children on earth. In a most personal way, Christ pleads for us before the Father: "Listen to him who is the advocate with the Father, who is pleading your cause before him—Saying: Father, behold the sufferings and death of him who did no sin, in whom thou wast well pleased; behold the blood of thy Son which was shed, the blood of him whom thou gavest that thyself might be glorified; Wherefore, Father, spare these my brethren that believe on my name, that they may come unto me and have everlasting life" (D&C 45:3–5).

The Lord's intervention on our behalf before the Father is expressed in lyric form in the following poem by Pamela Hamblin, based on the above passage:

THE ADVOCATE

Look upon the hands of Christ
That bear the pain past bearing;
Look upon the blood of One
Slaughtered for our sinning.

Apart, lamenting angels stand.
The Father weeps to watch Him die.
Earth in ash: the sundering quake
Of severed stone, shuddering sky.

The cup now poured, the burden borne,
God of Gethsemane knows our groans,
He stands before One whose plan He wrought
And tells at what cost our souls were bought.

> *Listen! for the gentle Son*
> *Pleads for us in Heavenly rooms.*
> *He shows his hands, the holy wounds,*
> *And bids the Father let us come.*[7]

The Lord does not plead our case on the basis of our own merits, but rather by virtue of his suffering on our behalf. We in turn must rely "wholly upon the merits of him who is mighty to save" (2 Nephi 31:19).[8]

The remission of sins is the central purpose of the Atonement, but its power and scope is not limited to payment for sin alone. As numerous scriptures make clear, the Lord Jesus Christ took upon himself not only the collective guilt of the world, but also its sicknesses, sorrows, injustices, and trials—every deleterious consequence of a fallen world. Elder Neal A. Maxwell has written: "Since not all human sorrow and pain is connected to sin, the full intensiveness of the Atonement involved bearing our pains, infirmities, and sicknesses, as well as our sins."[9] When tragedy takes place in our lives or illness strikes—physical, mental, or emotional—these are not necessarily the results of sin, but are the bitter fruits of a fallen world and the common lot of all mankind. Having experienced sickness and disappointment in his own life, our Savior can strengthen us in such trials as well. He is there for us not only when we cry out under the burden of sin, but also when we cry out from other forms of affliction as well.

The power of the Atonement also covers the sometimes terrible consequences of sin in the lives of innocent victims. An abused child, for example, may experience debilitating effects from maltreatment throughout his or her life—social troubles, low self-esteem, tendencies toward abuse, failure in temporal pursuits—but insofar as the child's agency is handicapped or limited as a result of the abuse, the Atonement of Christ will compensate for all of this with mercy. Through the infinite power of the Redemption, all will be made right in the here-after; there will be no injustice in the Day of Judgment, and no one will pay any eternal price for things over which they have no control. Similarly, the Atonement covers with redeeming power the innocent transgressions of those who are unac-countable for their own actions. Little children, the mentally handicapped, and all who are unaccountable for sin, will all be made "alive in Christ" (Moroni 8:22). He has taken the bur-dens of the innocent upon himself, with the promise that all will be made right in the end.

There is yet another dimension of Christ's redemptive power. The Lord Jesus Christ is our strength, support, and comfort in every weakness and trial, in every temptation and challenge of life. This is the full import of what it means to be a Savior—one who saves in every extremity. Whatever our problem, dilemma, or trial, he will be there, if we seek him. He is the "Bishop of your souls," (1 Peter 2:25), whose love and influence pervade all things. Not only is he the Great Mediator between God and man, he is a friend and stay in time of need.

This means that the Savior will not only cleanse us of past trespasses, but will help us overcome present weaknesses and endure daily temptations. The Lord teaches this plainly in the Book of Ether: "And if men come unto me I will show unto them their weakness. I give unto men weakness that they may be humble; and my grace is sufficient for all men that humble themselves before me; for if they humble themselves before me, and *have faith in me, then will I make weak things become strong unto them*" (Ether 12:27; emphasis added). His grace is sufficient to cover our intrinsic and inevitable shortcomings. If we exercise faith in him, he will strengthen us in temptation and, over time, turn our weakness into strength. The Savior taught this truth to the early elders of the Church: "Behold, and hearken, O ye elders of my church, saith the Lord your God, even Jesus Christ, your advocate, *who knoweth the weakness of man and how to succor them who are tempted*" (D&C 62:1; emphasis added).

In the fullest sense, then, the Atonement is the power whereby we are made strong in Christ and eventually can become perfect in him. His redeeming power can transform our very natures, turning moral and spiritual liabilities into assets. The Prince of Glory, as countless scriptures remind us, is he who:

- succors them who are tempted (D&C 62:1; Hebrews 2:18)
- out of weakness makes us strong (Hebrews 11:34)
- giveth power to the faint (Isaiah 40:29)
- makes a way to escape temptation (1 Cor. 10:13)
- makes us perfect in every good work (Hebrews 13:21)
- works a mighty change in us, or in our hearts (Mosiah 5:2)

All of which is what it means to "overcome by faith" (D&C 76:53). It is through faith in Christ that our sins are purged *and* our trials endured, our weaknesses made strong, our sorrows comforted.

The Atonement is sometimes regarded as a power that takes effect largely in the hereafter: we labor on our own in mortality to attain whatever degree of righteousness we can, and then the Atonement makes up the difference at the Judgment Day. Such a narrow conception ignores the imminent power of the Savior in our daily lives, here and now. The Atonement is not an abstract and impersonal balancing of mercy and justice that becomes effectual only at the Judgment Day. Rather, it is through the Savior that we gain strength to overcome the world and attain to any degree of righteousness. The Lord Jesus Christ is an ever-present strength, our strong arm, mainstay, and high tower in every hour of need. The Apostle Paul expressed this truth beautifully: "I can do all things through Christ which strengtheneth me" (Philippians 4:13).

THREE PERSONAL EXPERIENCES

The witness of the Holy Ghost that Jesus is the Christ and Savior of the world may be received countless times in a person's life. We may remember with particular intensity the first time that the Spirit bore testimony to our hearts, but there is nothing that prevents us from receiving that same confirming witness again and again. As Elder Jeffrey R. Holland writes: "In my lifetime I have had a thousand spiritual witnesses—ten thousand of them?—that Jesus is the Christ, the Everlasting Son of the Everlasting God."[10] Speaking for myself, I could not count how many times the Spirit of God has borne record to me of eternal truths; I only know that what the Spirit confirms once, it will confirm again, as need dictates. What follows are three personal experiences, each of which bore witness to me of the reality and redeeming mission of the Savior.

The doctrine of the Atonement kindled interest in me from an early age. As a young man only fifteen years old, I had many conversations with my father about the meaning of the Atonement and the balancing of justice and mercy. I remember feeling the warmth of the spirit during those talks, a quiet witness that Christ lives and is the Redeemer of the world. But though I had felt of the spirit, and believed in Christ, I did not really begin to understand the significance of the Atonement until my eighteenth year.

The year began in a difficult way. During the summer prior to my entering Brigham Young University, I worked as a laborer in a dairy factory in my hometown of Albuquerque, New Mexico. My coworkers were men of profane speech and worldly habits. Though I got along with them well enough, I was troubled by their language and graphic accounts of their exploits into sin. Fortunately, I spent much of my time alone in a large refrigerated room, stacking cases of cottage cheese that rolled in on a conveyor belt. Here in the cold and quiet there was time for reflection and prayer, and I found my testimony and faith growing with the passing weeks. I came to look forward each day to my quiet meditations in the cold. But, as is so often true in life, with every step forward in the Spirit there comes inevitable spiritual opposition from the adversary. I soon became aware of the adversary's influence pressing at the corners of my mind, an influence perhaps abetted by the coarseness of the environment in which I walked whenever I emerged from the storage room to labor with my coworkers.

When the summer ended, I sought a blessing from my father to help me cast from my mind the thoughts and feelings that sometimes troubled me. To my surprise, however, I sometimes continued to be troubled in a like manner even after leaving home for the university. The year ahead proved to be a year of spiritual struggle, as the influence of the adversary continued to press upon me, sometimes causing me to feel a sense of oppression from which I desperately wanted to, but could not entirely, flee. I sought guidance and help from many quarters—from the scriptures, from personal prayer, from study of the gospel, from service to others, from a kind and interested bishop—yet while each of these measures proved to be a blessing, none of them was adequate to win the spiritual struggle I faced.

Early in the year I was called to serve as a gospel doctrine teacher in my student ward. Because I had not been provided with a course manual, I selected my own topics and prepared my lessons from scratch. In the second half of the year, I decided to teach a series of lessons on Christ and his Redemption. One week I dedicated an entire Saturday afternoon and evening to preparing the next day's lesson. With so much time, I set about to read all of the principal discourses in the Book of Mormon on the subject of the Atonement, as well as related passages in the other standard works. I read passage after passage speaking of the triumph of the Savior, the plan of happiness, and the joy of the gospel. As I read, pure light seemed almost to diffuse from the pages of the scriptures. The power of the Spirit was overwhelming, and for the first time in my life, I saw the centrality of the Atonement in the plan of salvation.

Having spent many years fixated on the minutiae of gospel principles and commandments, and having often berated myself inordinately for my failure to live the letter of every imaginable command and counsel, sweet relief swept into my soul to realize that I had a Redeemer who loved me. He would stand by me, despite my shortcomings. As I read that day, I felt within the "peace of God, which passeth all understanding" (Philippians 4:7).

As the evening grew late, I read for at least the third time the following passage from Nephi:

"And now, my beloved brethren, after ye have gotten into this strait and narrow path, I would ask if all is done? Behold, I say unto you, Nay; for ye have not come thus far save it were by the word of Christ with unshaken faith in him, relying wholly upon the merits of him who is mighty to save.

"Wherefore, ye must press forward with a steadfastness in Christ, having a perfect brightness of hope, and a love of God and of all men. Wherefore, if ye shall press forward, feasting upon the word of Christ, and endure to the end, behold, thus saith the Father: Ye shall have eternal life.

"And now, behold, my beloved brethren, *this is the way;* and there is none other way nor name given under heaven whereby man can be saved in the kingdom of God. And now, behold, this is the doctrine of Christ, and the only and true doctrine of the Father, and of the Son, and of the Holy Ghost, which is one God, without end. Amen" (2 Nephi 31:19–21; emphasis added).

As I came to the phrase, "this is the way," I felt as though a heavenly hand had reached out to me. This was the end of my searching and struggle. The Lord Jesus Christ was in very deed *the way.* On that all-important evening of my life, the Holy Ghost bore witness to my heart that he is a living being, a present, tangible Redeemer on whom I could cast my burdens and in whom I could place my trust. He would be my strength in every trial and hour of need.

That testimony has been the guiding star of my life. It was not the first witness I ever received of the reality of Christ, nor was it the last, but it was surely the most powerful and important in terms of the direction and purpose it gave me. From that time forth, I could fairly say with Nephi, "I know in whom I have trusted" (2 Nephi 4:19). As for the spiritual opposition I had encountered, it diminished rapidly before the power of a newfound faith in the Redeemer, which gave me strength beyond my own.

The second experience I would share took place in 1987, in connection with a visit I made to Israel just a few days before Christmas. I was there on business, which was probably the only reason anyone visited the Holy Land that Christmas season. The Palestinian *intifada* had begun, the revolt of the local Arab population against Israeli rule, and the streets of Old Jerusalem were deserted. There was palpable political tension in the air, and to make matters worse, a cold rain drizzled down most of the week. The whole city bore a dreary aspect. Fearful of violence, the tourists stayed away in droves. Yet as I walked the streets of the city, umbrella in hand, peace filled my heart to know that this was the city he loved so much, the very place of his eternal sacrifice; to know that here had walked the Redeemer of both Jew and Gentile, Arab and Israeli, indeed of all mankind.

I returned to the United States late on a Saturday evening, just two days before Christmas. When the Sabbath dawned, my radio alarm awoke me to the music and words of "O Holy Night," with one passage that pierced me deeply: "The King of Kings lay thus in lowly manger, In all our trials born to be our friend."[11] Tears flowed as I contemplated the glorious sacrifice and perfect life of the Redeemer of Israel—he who was born the friend of the lowly and hope of the meek. Love flooded through my whole being for him who had come to earth and taken upon himself the burdens of us all. I was overwhelmed to think that he might regard me as a friend. I have never forgotten the tender feelings of that early Sunday morning, as pure a witness as I ever received.

I had a very different personal experience some years later that brought home to me the significance of the Savior's suffering in relieving our own trials. I was living with my family in Frankfurt, Germany, where I served in an area presidency of the Church. My kidneys were rapidly failing, causing intense discomfort. I knew that if the condition were not soon reversed, I would be forced to return to the United States for treatment, yet I was very reluctant to relinquish my assignment in the area presidency. One evening, I was attending a youth talent show at our local ward. I was in misery, both physically and spiritually—physically, because of the advancing kidney failure; spiritually, because I dreaded having to abandon my post and return to the United States. As I fought the pain, I suddenly cried out in my mind, "Why me, Lord? Why is this happening to me?" Anyone who has experienced a serious illness or accident has had reason to make the same cry. Examined at any moment of time, life can seem so unjust. Yet almost immediately a thought came to my mind, a quiet rebuke to my faithless murmur that I had not expected: "Yes, and why me? Why did I, who was sinless, have to suffer for your sins? Why was not the bitter cup withdrawn in that hour when I pleaded for mercy to the Father?"

My illness suddenly seemed a small thing; my doubts and

questions unworthy. The Master had endured far more than I would ever know, yet he alone among men deserved to suffer not at all. When he pleaded that the bitter cup be removed, he nevertheless said in all sincerity, "Thy will be done," and when the will of the Father was made manifest, he partook willingly and without complaint. What conceivable right, then, did I have to murmur or doubt the Lord's will? As I had feared, my deteriorating health did force my reassignment to the United States, and many months of treatment and surgery followed—but my perspective on that suffering was changed by the experience in the Church that evening. I would never suffer anything that Christ had not borne in far greater measure. With so great a captain as a friend, could not I bear my own trial in patience? These thoughts were a source of comfort to me in the weeks and months that followed.

CONCLUSION:
THE TESTIMONY OF A PRODIGAL

Rather than relate further experiences, I prefer to close this chapter with "pure testimony" (Alma 4:19). As a prodigal son who has accepted the ransom made by Jesus Christ, I add my own affirmation to "the many testimonies which have been given of him" (D&C 76:22). I know that he lives, that he is a real and tangible being, the very Son of God. He who was once known as Jesus of Nazareth stands enthroned in the heavens, a glorified and exalted personage far beyond man in every conceivable attribute of godliness. He is the Holy One of Israel, the Prince of Peace, the King of Kings. In his exalted station, he loves his people with a tenderness no less than he manifested in Galilee so long ago. I have felt his power; I have tasted of his love and grace. He is the one sure source of strength and solace in every extremity of life.

The beginning of wisdom is to acknowledge that we are prodigals, fallen offspring of an Eternal Father. Having strayed from his paths, we are wanderers on earth, sent forth to learn by experience that our only true home is with God. That lesson will be mastered only when we finally and permanently come unto Christ. As he declared: "I am Messiah, the King of Zion, the Rock of Heaven, which is broad as eternity; whoso cometh in at the gate and climbeth up by me shall never fall; wherefore, blessed are they of whom I have spoken, for they shall come forth with songs of everlasting joy" (Moses 7:53).

May we, through faith in him, be reconciled with our Father in Heaven and so return to our eternal home. A welcoming feast awaits us there.

CHAPTER FOUR

LIGHT OF
THE WORLD

The sun over the Mediterranean Sea receded slowly westward, casting shadows across the olive groves and hills east of Jerusalem. It was Passover Eve. The Galilean commoners meeting with Jesus of Nazareth for dinner in a large upper room that evening could not have known that their meal would someday be called the Last Supper. Had they known so, and why, they would have broken down in tears. The Paschal feast commenced under a cloud—the unmasking and banishment of the traitor Judas—but it ended in brilliant light, as Jesus revealed to them his true identity and mission. Things they had suspected, hoped for, and even intimated by the spirit, were revealed openly at last. Three of the Twelve had even been with him on the Mount of Transfiguration, but only now did they understand who he really was, this man with whom they had walked for three years: "Lo, now speakest thou plainly, and speakest no proverb. . . . By this we believe that thou camest forth from God" (John 16:29–30). He who stood before them was Messiah, the Son of God, the Light of the World.

As the gathering ended, Jesus offered the benediction, a

prayer of humble reverence that came to be known as the Great Intercessory Prayer. In the course of the prayer, he declared, "And this is life eternal, that they might know thee the only true God, and Jesus Christ, whom thou hast sent" (John 17:3). With these simple words the Savior taught that knowledge of God is the key to salvation, and that in order to know the Father, we must first come to know Christ, the intermediary between God and man, and the Father's anointed messenger to the world. "If ye had known me, ye should have known my Father also" (John 14:7). Knowing Christ is not only a prerequisite to salvation, but also the very essence of eternal life, for to know him is to be like him, and becoming like him is the whole object of the plan of salvation: "Beloved, now are we the sons of God, and it doth not yet appear what we shall be: but we know that, when he shall appear, we shall be like him; for we shall see him as he is" (1 John 3:2).

How can we come to know Christ as he really is? Three ways come to mind. The first is the purely spiritual dimension of *revelation*—knowledge of the living Christ that comes from trusting in him, praying in his name, and receiving inspiration and guidance from his spirit. "My sheep hear my voice" (John 10:27), he declared, and the better we heed that voice, the better we know the Master. The second way is that of *discipleship:* serving as he served. By acting as his true followers on the earth—feeding the hungry, visiting the sick, ministering to the poor—we come to know him by walking in the paths he walked. "For how knoweth a man the master whom he has not served, and who is a stranger unto him, and is far from the thoughts and intents of his heart?" (Mosiah 5:13). The third way to know Christ is by *study*, by reading and pondering the scriptural record of his life on earth. As the heaven-sent model of the perfect man, the embodiment of all virtue, we can hardly study his life and words enough. The New Testament gospels offer priceless accounts of his ministry and invaluable lessons about his personality, character, and transcendent greatness.

Of the latter, King David proclaimed, "Thine, O Lord, is the greatness" (1 Chronicles 29:11). The moral and spiritual stature of Christ tower over all eminent men of history, and none can claim to be his peer. Many volumes would be required to explore the greatness of the man Jesus in any detail, and no such treatise would be complete that did not include every conceivable attribute of goodness and godliness. Charles Edward Jefferson, pastor of the Broadway Tabernacle in New York City at the turn of the century, gave a classic set of sermons on "The Character of Jesus," later published in a book of the same name.[1] Jefferson identified twenty-three different qualities of the Savior and discoursed on each at length: strength, sincerity, reasonableness, poise, originality, narrowness, breadth, trust, brotherliness, optimism, chivalry, firmness, generosity, candor, enthusiasm, gladness, humility, patience, courage, indignation, reverence, holiness, and greatness. It is an impressive list, and Jefferson sifts the gospels with a fine sieve to examine each of these qualities in depth. But even this list is far from comprehensive, as its author acknowledges. We might add faith, hope, charity, integrity, wisdom, kindness, purity, boldness, gentleness, compassion, discernment, long-suffering, mercy, and a host of other virtues. Still the list would fall short. Perfection is impossible to compass in words.

My intention in the following pages is to discuss only a few qualities manifested in the Savior's life, seven in all, each taken from a specific period or event of his ministry. The objective is to let the majesty of him who was rightly called the "Light of the World" exalt our vision of what man can be. For as daunting as it may seem, we are explicitly commanded to be like him: "Therefore, what manner of men ought ye to be? Verily I say unto you, even as I am" (3 Nephi 27:27). To know the Savior, ultimately and eternally, we must become as he is: perfected in every virtue. It is a journey that will continue long after life is over, but for now there is no better place to gain understanding about what such perfection means than the New Testament.

HIS DILIGENCE: "ABOUT MY FATHER'S BUSINESS"

At the age of twelve, Jesus astounded a host of Rabbinical scholars in the temple at Jerusalem with his understanding of the law and the prophets. When Joseph and Mary, after a frantic two-day search for their missing son, finally found him in the temple, they chided him for causing them grief. Gently he turned away their concerns with the simple question: "Wist ye not that I must be about my Father's business?" (Luke 2:49). Even as a young boy, the Savior sought to be diligent in the work of God. Yet his response to his parents appears somewhat puzzling at first, since we know that his public ministry did not begin until the age of thirty, a full eighteen years after the incident in the temple. In what sense was he about his Father's business in the intervening, silent years, of which there is not even a single recorded deed or utterance?

68

The public ministry of the Master lasted but three years and was thus almost exactly a tithe of his life. We can hardly presume that the preceding nine-tenths of his life had no meaning for us or conveyed no message. Other than the account of his boyhood preaching in the temple, two brief phrases in the Gospels cover all we know of his life from the age of twelve to the age of thirty:

"Is not this the carpenter?" (Mark 6:3).[2]

"And Jesus increased in wisdom and stature, and in favour with God and man" (Luke 2:52).

These passages suggest at least two ways in which Jesus was about his Father's—and father's—business during those preparatory years in Nazareth: first, he pursued the chosen craft of his *legal father*, Joseph, the occupation of a carpenter; second, he prepared for service to his *Heavenly Father* by cultivating in himself the qualities of wisdom and virtue that would distinguish his mortal life to the end. On both accounts, his quiet diligence imparts a message to mankind as powerful and important as anything taught in his public ministry.

Those silent, preparatory years teach us that the lowly life of the laborer is good enough for God. As Saint Bonaventura observed, "His doing nothing wonderful was in itself a kind of wonder,"[3] for in living the life of a carpenter, he taught us that there is nothing to be ashamed of in manual labor, in obscurity, poverty, and the simple lot of ordinary people throughout the earth. Frederic Farrar stated this point eloquently in his masterful biography of the Savior: "Our Lord wished to show that labor is a pure and a noble thing; it is the salt of life; it is the girdle of manliness. . . . And therefore Christ labored, working with His own hands, and fashioned ploughs and yokes

69

for those who needed them . . . He came to teach that continual excitement, prominent action, distinguished services, brilliant success, are no essential elements of true and noble life, and that myriads of the beloved of God are to be found among the insignificant and the obscure."[4] Is there not here also a lesson about preparedness? The greatest man who ever lived took time—long years of time—to lay a foundation of learning and personal growth before undertaking his life's mission. "And I, John, saw that he received not of the fulness at the first, but received grace for grace . . . until he received a fulness" (D&C 93:12–13). To work, to prepare, to wait—all these may seem mundane and ordinary, but the Son of Man devoted years to such labor as he took upon himself the common yoke of all mankind.

HIS VITALITY: "I AM COME THAT THEY MIGHT HAVE LIFE"

He loved life, he imparted light, and his mission was to serve as the Life and Light of the World. "The thief cometh not, but for to steal, and to kill, and to destroy: I am come that they might have life, and that they might have it more abundantly" (John 10:10). No man ever lived who loved life more richly, more fully, with more unbridled joy than he.

To begin with, he loved the vitality of nature. Time and again Christ sought solace in the outdoors: in the green hills west of Galilee, the fields and meadows surrounding Jerusalem, the rural byways outside Nazareth. "All his days were spent in the open air."[5] His parables, replete with allusions to the intricacies of the plant and animal kingdoms, reflected his love of all things living. For a carpenter, he possessed an astonishing array of knowledge about the flora and fauna of Palestine, knowledge that could only have come from intimate observation and experience. The Savior's love of nature was particularly evident in the last week of his life, when he retired each evening from the noise and squalor of Jerusalem to the pastoral village of Bethany: Here in the fresh air of the hills, surrounded by portentous olive groves, it is likely that he could more readily find communion with his Father as he prepared for the cup to come.

Jesus loved not only the living creations of the natural world, but also the life and vibrancy of human society, of which he ever seemed to be the center. Why else would the Gospel writers spend so much time recalling the many dinners and feasts he attended: from the wedding at Cana to the feast at Matthew's home in Capernaum; from his reception at the home of Zacchaeus in Jericho to the dinner with Mary and Martha in Bethany; from the feast with Simon the Pharisee in that same village to the Last Supper with his disciples. And this list does not include numerous other occasions: the Passover and other feasts in Jerusalem, implied but not detailed in the Gospels; his feeding of the four and five thousand; his numerous travels abroad with his disciples, supping and commingling with people all around. All strata of Judaean society clamored for his presence. "And one of the Pharisees desired him that he would eat with him" (Luke 7:36). "And as he spake, a certain Pharisee besought him to dine with him" (Luke 11:37). As Bruce Barton observes, "No other public figure ever had a more interesting list of friends. It ran from the top of the social ladder to the bottom."[6]

Those who would turn religion into a cold and somber

enterprise, devoid of human warmth, will find no encouragement from the Life of the World. Those who would condemn the simple pleasures of daily life, the gaiety of social occasions, or the inevitable inefficiencies of friendship as somehow unbecoming or impious are straying perilously close to the camp of the Pharisees. The way to discern the path of life from all other paths is quite simple: "Every thing which inviteth and enticeth to do good, and to love God, and to serve him, is inspired of God" (Moroni 7:13). All that comes from Christ is wholesome and life-bringing; all that comes from beneath is death.

HIS COURAGE: "FEAR NOT"

His ministry was overshadowed by violence, steeped in controversy, and conducted in a whirlwind of chaos and action: "I came not to send peace, but a sword" (Matthew 10:34). His words divided father from son, brother from brother, and ruler from ruled. All men sought after him, the whole world was turned upside down by him, and he left Palestine and all of mankind forever changed by the revolutionary dynamism of his doctrine. Yet for all this, his personal life was an oasis of calm; his ministry best characterized by quiet days in Capernaum and Galilee. His first words of counsel to his newly called disciples were simply, "Fear not" (Luke 5:10). Serenity and profound peace reigned in him continually, even in moments of dire danger or the most chaotic controversy. A man of undaunted courage, he could not be shaken.

The whole imposing religious establishment of the Kingdom of Judaea stood arrayed against Jesus: the scribes, the Rabbis, the Pharisees, the Sadducees, the Sanhedrin. Normally at odds with one another, they united in conspiracy and hatred against him, this obscure carpenter from Nazareth. They stalked him mercilessly, twisted his words, slandered his name, scorned his teachings, and sought his life. Cunningly and without scruple they manipulated their Roman overlords against him. When they finally dragged him before justice, so-called, they would countenance no mercy, but insisted on inflicting upon him the most excruciating death known to man. Through it all, he neither wavered nor flinched. We cannot detect the slightest trace of fear in his actions or words from the beginning of his ministry to his death on the cross. He met every accusation with silent serenity, faced every danger with equanimity. Even in the face of the most bitter invective, he never compromised his teachings, his mission, or his manhood. He did not hesitate to denounce the hypocrisy of the scribes and Pharisees, even knowing that this would only fuel the mounting fire. So legendary was his strength of character, his valor, that when a legion of Roman soldiers came to apprehend him in Gethsemane, they fell backward at the very revelation of his person (John 18:6).

Nothing reveals his courage more plainly than the twice-fold cleansing of the temple. It was profoundly significant that he cleansed the temple precincts not once, but twice. The first cleansing took place early in his ministry, when he was still unknown and unheralded (John 2:14–16). Who was this stranger with the audacity to overthrow tables and chase away money-changers, to interfere so brashly with business that had been conducted in this manner for decades? We read of no opposition to his actions, however. His majesty and sheer physical presence must have intimidated every potential foe.

The Rabbinic overseers of the temple could hardly protest his actions, for the money-changing was plainly illegal and blasphemous; the cleansing was nevertheless the beginning of his rift with the Jewish establishment.

The second cleansing of the temple is even more instructive (Matthew 21:12–16; Mark 11:15–19; Luke 19:45–48). It came at the end of Christ's ministry and sent an uncompromising message of his determination to defend the sanctity of the house of God, regardless of human opinion or possible retribution. Now, when opposition was mounting and his every action scrutinized for possible criminal implications, he did not hesitate to despoil the money-changers again, displaying not only courage, but undeviating integrity and consistency as well. No political calculation or fear of reprisal could change his course by one iota, despite overwhelming odds against him. The Master did what was right in every circumstance and regardless of consequence. In him, righteousness and fearlessness met and became one.

HIS LONELINESS: "OF THE PEOPLE, THERE WAS NONE WITH ME"

He walked with multitudes, yet ever seemed to walk alone. His former neighbors in Nazareth sought to take his life; his closest disciples did not understand him; and his friends abandoned him in the last hours of his life. Loneliness was his constant companion. This has always been true of great men, but never more intensely than with Christ. "The foxes have holes, and the birds of the air have nests; but the Son of man hath not where to lay his head" (Matthew 8:20).

One might object that loneliness is not a character trait, but simply a condition or state of mind. This is true enough, but loneliness builds character in those who master its formidable weight; it is a teacher of patience and fortitude. The Savior's forbearance in loneliness, his willingness to forsake the crowd and his determination to do what was right, no matter who walked with him—all these were enduring character traits of the Lord Jesus Christ. All stemmed in part from the often solitary path he walked in life.

Sociable and gregarious as Jesus was, his loneliness was not primarily that of physical isolation, but rather the fruit of misunderstanding and rejection. He was always different, set apart, and misinterpreted, even by his closest disciples. "Have I been so long time with you, and yet hast thou not known me?" (John 14:9), the Savior asked Philip at the Last Supper. He might have asked the same of any of the disciples. Perhaps it was inevitable that they would misunderstand him throughout most of his ministry. His identity as the Son of God, his role as Creator, the infinite burden he would yet carry—these were concepts far removed from Judaic understanding, so exalted in conception that he could only hint at them from time to time, never sharing them fully until the Last Supper. Until the very end, he bore his greatest burdens alone.

Nor was it his disciples alone who failed to comprehend him. His whole ministry was one of rejection: "He is despised and rejected of men . . . and we hid as it were our faces from him" (Isaiah 53:3). In the halcyon days of his early ministry, it appeared he might gather all Judaea unto him: "All men seek for thee," said his disciples (Mark 1:37). But the trend of events was soon decidedly downhill, as one by one, groups who once had expressed allegiance rejected him and turned away.

His hometown of Nazareth could never see beyond his humble origins; angered by his claims and teachings, they rejected him twice, once seeking to throw him from the brow of a hill. Capernaum, where he lived for many months and performed many of his greatest miracles, found his presence an inconvenience and turned its back on him. Shortly later, when he made clear to the crowds massed around him that his mission was spiritual and he had not come to win political or temporal salvation for Israel, many of his closest disciples "walked no more with him" (John 6:66). Finally, one of the Twelve, a close companion through most of his ministry, sold him for a few pieces of silver. He knew what it was to be an outcast, repeatedly tossed aside as "a thing of naught" (1 Nephi 19:9), until in the end only John the Beloved and a few weeping women huddled beneath his rain-drenched cross.

Rejection by friends and society was no doubt painful for a man as gregarious and loving as Jesus. Yet it was only a foretaste of the far more soul-rending loneliness he would experience in Gethsemane. In previous hours of lonely vigil, the Father had always been near. But in the ordeal of that night, even the Father withdrew his spirit, leaving Christ cut off from every source of aid or solace—this that he might work out the atoning sacrifice by his own power alone. Of that descent below all things, the scriptures say simply, "there was none to help" (Isaiah 63:5). Those five words might serve as an epitaph of his whole life.

"He came unto his own, and his own received him not" (John 1:11). Because the Savior was abandoned and rejected, because he suffered estrangement even from the spirit, he understands intimately the sorrows of those who are spurned or ignored, of all who struggle alone against the darkness of the world. He has vowed that his sheep will never be abandoned: "I will not leave you comfortless: I will come to you" (John 14:18). With the King of Kings as a friend and stay, God's children on earth need never walk alone.

HIS HUMANITY: "THE SON OF MAN CAME EATING AND DRINKING"

A spurious image of the man Jesus has come down to us through the centuries: an image of Christ as weak, pale, austere, and somehow inhuman and otherworldly. Transmitted by religious art and writings, this image originated both from the Greek idealism that pervaded the larger Mediterranean world of the early Christian era and from medieval monasticism. The former popularized the notion that all things physical and human were imperfect, crude shadows of a more ideal sphere; while the latter sought refuge from the world in the ascetic life of the cold monastery, hard bed, and hair shirt. Christian theologians from Augustine onward could not entirely escape these influences, and so they often pictured Christ as anything but warm and human.

But they were wrong, as even a cursory examination of the Gospels makes plain. *The Son of Man was a man*, though also divine, and he partook of and enjoyed the pleasures of life in full abundance, knowing that they were gifts of God and sanctioned by the Almighty, so long as they were enjoyed in temperance and within the bounds of God's laws. Perhaps nowhere is this more plain than in Christ's extended eulogy of John the Baptist in the eleventh chapter of Matthew, a portion of which reads: "But whereunto shall I liken this

77

generation? It is like unto children sitting in the markets, and calling unto their fellows, and saying, We have piped unto you, and ye have not danced; we have mourned unto you, and ye have not lamented. For John came neither eating nor drinking, and they say, He hath a devil. The Son of man came eating and drinking, and they say, Behold a man gluttonous, and a winebibber, a friend of publicans and sinners" (vv. 11:16–19).

John the Baptist was a man of austerity, living in the wilderness in rough raiment, surviving on locusts and wild honey. A harbinger of justice and judgment, he was a God-sent messenger of the strictness of the law, the narrowness of the path, and the unyielding perfectness of God's ways. Jesus, by contrast— though unsullied and perfect in every point of the Mosaic law—came as the giver of a higher law, as a herald of mercy, joy, and love. He came singing and dancing, eating and drinking, a man of warmth and full-blooded humanity. It was precisely his warmth, joviality, and free-spirited mingling with commoners that won him the opprobrium of the Judaean establishment. For a long time, the worst they could say of him was "he eateth and drinketh with publicans and sinners" (Mark 2:16).

Ironically, the scribes and Pharisees could accept neither John nor Jesus—John, because he reminded them of their sins and imperfections under the exacting standards of their own legal code; Jesus, because his warmth and humanity shed such vivid light on the narrow-minded hypocrisy of their ways. Nothing more perturbs the Pharisee than a warmhearted spirit, and the Master radiated joy in his daily walk among the people. Yet he was also a man of sorrows, who felt deeply the pain of the impoverished and the sick, and who suffered private anguish for the sins of his people. The heights of his joy paralleled the depths of his sorrow. Contrast his accusers: knowing no real human joy, they did not comprehend human suffering. Having never tasted the happiness of life, love, and friendship, they could not understand the sorrows of those who genuinely care. It was they who were inhuman; how ironic, then, that they should accuse him of having a devil! (John 10:20).

Nothing reflects Christ's understanding of basic human needs more perfectly than his attitude toward the Sabbath Day. He was Lord of the Sabbath, the Law-giver who on Mount Sinai had proclaimed the seventh day to be holy. Not in the slightest point did he ever violate the sanctity of that day; to the contrary, he sanctified it all the more through serving, healing, and administering; for these acts of love the Pharisees pilloried him. True enough, he ignored the hundreds of petty rules, interpretations, emendations, and regulations by which they had turned the Sabbath into a veritable *Rameumpton* of fastidious self-righteousness. In trying to build fences around the simple law of the Torah, the scribes had completely forgotten the spirit and intent of the Sabbath day, which for them had become principally an opportunity to catch one's neighbor in violation. Such a Sabbath would serve only to shrink and warp human souls, and Jesus would have nothing to do with it, declaring instead, "The sabbath was made for man, and not man for the sabbath" (Mark 2:27). For the Savior, the whole gospel was meant for man. He never valued rules and principles above the worth of human souls.

HIS HUMILITY: "FOR I AM MEEK AND LOWLY IN HEART"

During the latter part of his ministry, as the Savior traveled through "the coasts of Judaea" and the province known as Perea, he made a remarkable declaration about himself: "Come unto me, all ye that labour and are heavy laden, and I will give you rest. Take my yoke upon you, and learn of me; *for I am meek and lowly in heart:* and ye shall find rest unto your souls" (Matthew 11:28–29; emphasis added). Only a truly humble man can honestly declare his own humility. The proud cannot do so without manifest hypocrisy, nor would they be so inclined, since pride places little value on humility. In this instance, Christ reassured his listeners that they could freely cast their burdens—even their most intimate and painful burdens—upon him, for his meekness was such that he would never embarrass, criticize, or reject them. He would simply minister to them in humility, helping them find inner peace.

Humility is etched in every setting and deed of the life of Christ. Instead of worldly station, he chose the simple life of a carpenter and itinerant preacher. He grew up in an obscure village located in a despised province of Judaea. He had no social status, but spent his ministry associating with fishermen, peasants, publicans, and sinners, mingling freely with the outcast of the earth. He eschewed high office and political power, though many of his disciples urged it on him. He held forth a little child as an ensample for those who would enter the kingdom of heaven. Even the high point of his ministry, the triumphal entry into Jerusalem, was a simple, almost homespun, affair by worldly standards: "Behold, thy King cometh unto thee, meek, and sitting upon an ass, and a colt the foal of an ass" (Matthew 21:5, see also Zechariah 9:9). Jesus was sinless in every point, yet when a follower called him "Good Master," he replied, "Why callest thou me good? there is none good but one, that is, God" (Matthew 19:17). Throughout his ministry, he never took glory unto himself, but rendered all glory and praise to the Father.

Christ's humility was not the weak and self-abasing trait so often portrayed in literature and art. It was quite the contrary, as Joseph Smith taught in Nauvoo: "Some of the company thought I was not a very meek Prophet; so I told them: 'I am meek and lowly in heart,' and will personify Jesus for a moment, to illustrate the principle, and cried out with a loud voice, 'Woe unto you, ye doctors; woe unto you, ye lawyers; woe unto you, ye scribes, Pharisees, and hypocrites!' But you cannot find the place where I ever went that I found fault with [the Saints'] food, their drink, their house, their lodgings; no, never; and this is what is meant by the meekness and lowliness of Jesus."[7] The Son of God did not deign himself so high as to shun the company of the most ordinary people. His intermingling in their society—partaking of their food and drink, visiting their homes—was a key facet of his meekness and a source of his matchless power over human hearts.

Particularly instructive is the parable of the Pharisee and the publican, in which Christ contrasts the self-justifying prayer of a Pharisee with the self-effacing prayer of a publican. Both men went to the temple to pray. The Pharisee prayed words of self-approval, "God, I thank thee, that I am not as other men are, extortioners, unjust, adulterers, or even as this publican. I fast twice in the week, I give tithes of all that I possess" (Luke

18:11–12). The publican would not even lift up his eyes to heaven, but smote himself upon his breast and prayed, "God be merciful to me a sinner" (Luke 18:13). The Savior declares, "I tell you, this man went down to his house justified rather than the other: for every one that exalteth himself shall be abased; and he that humbleth himself shall be exalted" (Luke 18:14). The publican's prayer was that of the genuinely penitent everywhere; it is the prayer all must offer if the Atonement is to find effect in their lives.

The scriptures make clear that the humility of Christ was not a characteristic of his mortal life only, but an eternal virtue as well, a fundamental attribute of godliness. The Father spoke of his dwelling place with the Son in these terms: "For thus saith the high and lofty One that inhabiteth eternity, whose name is Holy; I dwell in the high and holy place, *with him also that is of a contrite and humble spirit*, to revive the spirit of the humble, and to revive the heart of the contrite ones" (Isaiah 57:15; emphasis added). Consider also Moroni's testimony of his personal audience with the Savior: "And then shall ye know that I have seen Jesus, and that he hath talked with me face to face, and that *he told me in plain humility*, even as a man telleth another in mine own language, concerning these things" (Ether 12:39; emphasis added). The Savior's visitation to Moroni took place more than three centuries after the resurrection of Christ; Moroni was not testifying of Christ the mortal, but of Christ, the Eternal God of heaven and earth. The Apostle Paul, who knew Christ only as a resurrected being, testified similarly of "the meekness and gentleness of Christ" (2 Corinthians 10:1) and of "the simplicity that is in Christ" (2 Corinthians 11:3).

As Jesus Christ was meek and lowly in heart, so also will be every heir to the Kingdom of God. The cardinal attribute required at the Judgment Day will be a broken heart and a contrite spirit, for "unto none else can the ends of the law be answered" (2 Nephi 2:7). As David declared, "The Lord is nigh unto them that are of a broken heart; and saveth such as be of a contrite spirit" (Psalm 34:18). A broken heart and a contrite spirit entails sacrifice, because it means jettisoning all pride, self-justification, and worldliness in order to give our hearts fully and without condition to God. Again from the Psalmist: "The sacrifices of God are a broken spirit: a broken and a contrite heart, O God, thou wilt not despise" (Psalm 51:17). Christ declared this same doctrine when he announced the advent of a new law, transcending the Mosaic law, to the Nephites in Bountiful: "Your sacrifices and your burnt offerings shall be done away, for I will accept none of your sacrifices and your burnt offerings. *And ye shall offer for a sacrifice unto me a broken heart and a contrite spirit*" (3 Nephi 9:19–20; emphasis added).

Had the Savior not been meek and lowly of heart, he could hardly have brought to pass the Atonement, for its accomplishment required that he humble himself beneath every indignity, including death itself. As Paul wrote of the Master, "being found in fashion as a man, he humbled himself, and became obedient unto death, even the death of the cross" (Philippians 2:8). By submitting to the will of the Father in all things, Christ became, like the Father, the master of all things. His meekness made possible the eternal Atonement. His humility purchased our salvation.

HIS SERVANTSHIP: "BUT HE THAT IS GREATEST AMONG YOU SHALL BE YOUR SERVANT"

Isaiah lived more than seven centuries before Christ, yet he knew of the Savior's ordeal on the cross and many other details of his mortal life. His prophetic writings portray Jesus as the Suffering Servant, one who came to serve his Father and his Father's children, and who, in serving, experienced suffering. "Behold my servant, whom I have chosen; my beloved, in whom my soul is well pleased" (Matthew 12:18, citing Isaiah 42:1). The crowning example of both servantship and suffering was the Great Atonement itself, in which he voluntarily took upon himself the sins of all human beings in order that they might not have to endure the suffering he bore. But service, in all its myriad forms, was the watchword of his life, pervading all he did. It was an outward manifestation of the pure love that filled his being.

In his testimony to Cornelius, Peter summed up the life of Christ in a simple, but telling phrase: "Jesus of Nazareth . . . *went about doing good*" (Acts 10:38; emphasis added). We will never know all the good he did. The New Testament Gospels record more than thirty distinct instances of Christ having healed, raised from the dead, or cast out spirits from specific individuals, identified by name or circumstance. There are also several accounts of his ministering to more purely spiritual needs, providing comfort and counsel to such persons as Nicodemus, the Samaritan woman, the rich young ruler, the woman taken in adultery, Mary Magdalene, Zacchaeus, and— again and again—to his apostles. These accounts, however, constitute only a minute fraction of Christ's three-year ministry of service. Many passages read like this one from the Gospel of Matthew: "And great multitudes came unto him, having with them those that were lame, blind, dumb, maimed, and many others, and cast them down at Jesus' feet; and he healed them" (Matthew 15:30). John the Beloved tried to capture the magnitude of his good works with the tribute that concludes his Gospel: "And there are also many other things which Jesus did, the which, if they should be written every one, I suppose that even the world itself could not contain the books that should be written" (John 21:25).

Jesus demonstrated the meaning of servantship at the time of the Last Supper, when he girded himself with a towel, poured water in a basin, and washed his disciples' feet. Peter, ever brash, resisted the washing until the Lord informed him: "If I wash thee not, thou hast no part with me" (John 13:8). No doubt the other disciples, though silent, were also discomfited to have their feet washed by the Master. Clearly Jesus acted with the most sacred and divine intentions, one of which was to teach a lesson of supreme importance:

"Know ye what I have done to you?

"Ye call me Master and Lord: and ye say well; for so I am.

"If I then, your Lord and Master, have washed your feet; ye also ought to wash one another's feet.

"For I have given you an example, that ye should do as I have done to you" (John 13:12–15).

Even the Lord of heaven and earth did not deem himself too high to serve his brethren in a simple way. For him, *lordship was servantship.* The highest of all was the servant of all.

In Luke's account of the Last Supper, the same lesson is taught in a different context. Luke does not mention the washing of the feet, but he does say that "a strife" arose among the disciples as to who among them should be accounted the greatest:

"And he said unto them, The kings of the Gentiles exercise lordship over them; and they that exercise authority upon them are called benefactors.

"But ye shall not be so: but he that is greatest among you, let him be as the younger; and he that is chief, as he that doth serve.

"For whether is greater, he that sitteth at meat, or he that serveth? is not he that sitteth at meat? But I am among you as he that serveth" (Luke 22:25–27).

In the eyes of the world, the man who presides at the head of a table and is served is clearly the greatest. But Christ, the greatest of all, would have nothing to do with this viewpoint. "I am among you as he that serveth."

Returning to the account of the Last Supper in the Gospel of John, it is instructive to follow the Savior's exchange with the ever petulant Peter: "Peter saith unto him, Thou shalt never wash my feet. Jesus answered him, If I wash thee not, thou hast no part with me. Simon Peter saith unto him, Lord, not my feet only, but also my hands and my head" (John 13:8–9). The Master's reply to Peter is not merely an admonition of the moment, but a foreshadowing of the Atonement and a statement of doctrinal truth: no one who is not washed by Christ shall enter the kingdom of heaven. But there is a more mundane lesson here also: we must learn to receive service, as well as to give it. For some, that is the harder task. In the kingdom of God, all are servants, yet all are served.

In the book of Matthew, Christ speaks of the Judgment Day,

when the King shall divide the nations into sheep and goats, with the sheep on his right hand. Then the King shall say unto them on his right hand: "Come, ye blessed of my Father, inherit the kingdom prepared for you from the foundation of the world: For I was an hungred, and ye gave me meat: I was thirsty, and ye gave me drink: I was a stranger, and ye took me in: naked, and ye clothed me: I was sick, and ye visited me: I was in prison, and ye came unto me" (Matthew 25:34–36). The righteous shall protest that they did none of these things, to which the King shall reply: "Verily I say unto you, *Inasmuch as ye have done it unto one of the least of these my brethren, ye have done it unto me*" (Matthew 25:40; emphasis added).

To serve the least among our fellowman is to serve the Lord, who made himself least for the sake of the lowly. Such service is the fruit of charity, "the pure love of Christ" (Moroni 7:47), without which all things must fail. Upon those who follow in his footsteps, Christ will bestow the same sacred title by which he was known in ancient prophecy, that of *Servant:* "Well done, thou good and faithful servant: thou hast been faithful over a few things, I will make thee ruler over many things: enter thou into the joy of thy lord" (Matthew 25:21). No higher accolade can be given to any disciple of Christ.

CONCLUSION: THE PERFECT MAN

"Mark the perfect man, and behold the upright" (Psalm 37:37). The Psalmist doubtless had the promised Messiah in mind, the one perfect and wholly upright man. He was the "lamb without blemish and without spot" (1 Peter 1:19). He was "in all points tempted like as we are, yet without sin"

87

(Hebrews 4:15). Here was a man so holy that when a suffering woman touched the hem of his garment in a crowd, he knew it instantly, "for I perceive that virtue is gone out of me" (Luke 8:46).[8] He who called himself "The Way" showed us the way of virtue in every point. Without the life of Christ, the world would have no adequate definition of perfection.

We are accustomed to thinking of Jesus as perfect in act and deed. We should remember that he was also perfect *in mind and word*. His was the superior intellect of all human history. Already at the age of twelve he had surpassed the wisdom of the great Rabbinical minds of his day, who were "astonished at his understanding and answers" (Luke 2:47). Later in his ministry, astonishment would be a common response to his teachings. When the Pharisees in Jerusalem sent officers of the law to arrest him, they returned empty-handed, with the excuse, "Never man spake like this man" (John 7:46). His every word was flawless, his response to every accuser incisive and irrefutable. "He stripped off the accidental from the soul of the essential, and no matter how tangled or complicated a matter was he seized the dominant principle and made all things plain."[9] His answers to the most difficult questions posed him have come down through history as classics of verbal rhetoric:

- Render unto Caesar that which is Caesar's (Matthew 22:21; Mark 12:17; Luke 20:25).

- Let he who is without sin cast the first stone (John 8:7).

- The sabbath was made for man and not man for the sabbath (Mark 2:27).

- If a kingdom be divided against itself, that kingdom cannot stand (Mark 3:24).

In the end, after repeated attempts to confound him, his

adversaries gave up in frustration: "And no man was able to answer him a word, neither durst any man from that day forth ask him any more questions" (Matthew 22:46). He who was *The Word* was a master of words, a wellspring of wisdom and truth.

"His name shall be called Wonderful," wrote Isaiah, capturing in one word the overwhelming sense of awe with which we contemplate the Savior's life. "If Shakespeare was to come into this room," said Charles Lamb, "we should all rise up to meet him; but if Christ was to come into it, we should all fall upon our knees."[10] His greatness and majesty are of a wholly different order than that of all other great men of history. His virtues are full-bodied in every point, his character of diamond purity, his life and being the soul of beauty. Nothing can be added to his perfection.

Jesus Christ was the Light of the World before his birth, the Bright and Morning Star. He was the Light of the World when he walked upon his footstool as Immanuel and Son of Man. And he is the Light of the World today and forever, the Eternal God, whose power, influence, and spirit pervade all space: "the light which is in all things, which giveth life to all things, which is the law by which all things are governed, even the power of God who sitteth upon his throne, who is in the bosom of eternity, who is in the midst of all things" (D&C 88:13). The great promise, last of all, is that the righteous shall see him and know of a surety that he is the Only Begotten of the Father and the light that is in them: "Then shall ye know that ye have seen me, that I am, and that I am the true light that is in you, and that you are in me; otherwise ye could not abound" (D&C 88:50).

CHAPTER FIVE

THE PRICE OF RANSOM

The evangelists Matthew and Mark each record the Savior's declaration that he came "to give his life a ransom for many" (Matthew 20:28; Mark 10:45). A ransom traditionally denotes that a price is paid, a sum of money or gold, either to purchase a captive's freedom from bondage or to release a debtor from a hopeless and unpayable debt. More rarely, there have been instances in history of brave men offering their very lives in exchange for their fellow soldiers who faced execution or were held as prisoners of war. The Atonement of Christ combined all of these elements: he ransomed mankind from the bondage of sin; he paid an unpayable debt; and he offered his life to free God's children from the captivity of death.

How costly was that ransom? At what price did the Savior rescue the world from death and hell? When the Son of Man descended below all things and drank of the bitter cup, how long was the draught and how sore his sorrows? These questions merit pondering even if the answers will not be known fully in this life. Reflection on the Master's suffering illuminates the magnitude of God's love for his children. As we come to realize what a high price Christ paid for our salvation—that he bore all things freely and willingly on our behalf—that realization will kindle in us a deeper devotion to the Son of God. As John the Beloved affirmed: "We love him, because he first loved us" (1 John 4:19).

None of this is to advocate dwelling excessively on the suffering of the Savior. We do not display crucifixes in our chapels precisely because we prefer not to emphasize his pains and his death, but rather his triumph over them, the joy of redemption and hope of the resurrection. The assurance of his ultimate victory substitutes rejoicing for grief and "the oil of joy for mourning" (Isaiah 61:3). Nevertheless, we have covenanted to "always remember him" (D&C 20:79), which covenant the prophets have plainly taught includes memory of his suffering. Such remembrance may also bring consolation as we bear our own crosses through life—for even as Christ suffered to more perfectly know us, we suffer sometimes to better know him.

In simple quantitative terms, the only measure of the Redeemer's ransom that will ever suffice is contained in the scriptural phrase, "infinite and eternal" (Alma 34:14). The suffering of the Savior was beyond all human measure, the price of his ransom uncountable:

> *See, the Good Shepherd is seeking,*
> *Seeking the lambs that are lost,*
> *Bringing them in with rejoicing,*
> *Saved at such infinite cost.*[1]

Amulek in his great sermon to the Zoramites on the Atonement taught that anything less than an infinite ransom would have fallen short of the demands of justice. Moreover, said Amulek, not only did Christ bear an infinite burden of pain and grief as he wrought out the Atonement, but it was

91

necessary that he himself *be* Infinite and Eternal in order to accomplish it (Alma 34:9–14). A finite being could not bear an infinite weight.

What did paying the price of our ransom mean in stark, immediate reality for the Son of God? What did Jesus have to endure in Gethsemane, at Golgotha, and at other times of his life, in order to ransom mankind from death and hell?

THE PRICE OF A PERFECT LIFE

We are accustomed to saying that the Atonement took place in Gethsemane. In a literal sense this is true, since it was in Gethsemane that Christ took upon himself the full burden and weight of the sins of the world. But the trial of Jesus in Gethsemane would not have been possible and could not have occurred had it not been preceded by a lifetime of sinless virtue, accomplished in the face of the most vehement spiritual opposition. From his temptation in the wilderness to his rejection in Nazareth to the illegal trial before the Sanhedrin, Christ paid the price of a perfect life, walking in holy sinlessness despite adversity, physical suffering, deep sorrows, and the snares of ruthless and determined adversaries, both seen and unseen. "He suffered temptations but gave no heed unto them" (D&C 20:22). All this he did with the knowledge that one misstep would mean creation's doom! For had he sinned even in the smallest point or slightest negligence of thought, the Atonement would have become impossible and the whole purpose of creation frustrated. The burden of the whole world weighed upon him through every moment of his life. He was

God's fulcrum, the divine pivot around which the hopes of eternity revolved.

Christ's suffering culminated in Gethsemane, but it did not begin there. Alma prophesied that after his birth Christ would "go forth, suffering pains and afflictions and temptations *of every kind*; and this that the word might be fulfilled which saith he will take upon him the pains and the sicknesses of his people" (Alma 7:11; emphasis added). Plainly this prophecy applied not only to Gethsemane and Calvary, but to his whole mortal life. The magnitude of adversity he would face in life first became clear during the temptation in the wilderness, when, weakened by hunger and thirst, the Savior was compelled to face the full cunning of the Tempter himself. From then to the end of his life, Lucifer spared no energy in mounting one onslaught after another against the Holy One. His afflictions and trials "of every kind" were all-encompassing in both scope and intensity.

Alma's words, cited above, about Christ taking upon himself "the pains and the sicknesses of his people," intimate that Jesus was no stranger to infirmities of the body, including ordinary human illness. While there is no specific account in the scriptures of Jesus falling sick, this too must have been among the afflictions he bore, like almost all human beings at sometime in their life. He did not take upon him our sicknesses in an abstract sense alone; he tasted and knew what it meant to be borne down by infirmity. Christ also knew what it was to be despised and rejected by his fellowman. He bore the scorn and opprobrium of society all his life. In one who loved so much, the sting of rejection must have wounded deeply, which may be why Isaiah, despite Christ's native warmth and cheerful nature, saw him as "a man of sorrows, and acquainted with grief" (Isaiah 53:3).

The trials and temptations Jesus experienced throughout his life were a necessary prelude to what happened in Gethsemane, part of his preparation to partake of the bitter cup. To suppose otherwise would be to say that only the last week of his life was pertinent to the Atonement. No, it all mattered, it all weighed in the balance; his whole life, filled with trials, was an integral part of his role as Redeemer. "For it became him, for whom are all things, and by whom are all things . . . to make the captain of their salvation perfect through sufferings" (Hebrews 2:10). Tried by every conceivable fire and dart of the adversary, sinless and unsullied, Christ could come to the Last Supper and declare in all humility to his disciples, "Be of good cheer; I have overcome the world" (John 16:33). Only after subduing all worldly things did he become a fit offering for the altar of God. Refined in the fire of life, he was prepared for Gethsemane.

A TRIAL OF THE SPIRIT: THE BITTER CUP OF GETHSEMANE

Gethsemane was a garden, an olive grove, situated on the west side of the Mount of Olives, across the brook Kidron from the walled city of Jerusalem. Though its exact location is not known today, legend holds that it was not far up the hillside, probably less than three hundred yards from the floor of the ravine that runs between the eastern walls of Jerusalem and the famous Mount. Groves of olive trees still cover much of that portion of the mountain today, so it is not difficult for a visitor to get a sense of the place to which Christ and his disciples retired following the Last Supper. The name Gethsemane stems from the Hebrew words *Gat*, meaning "press," and *Shemen*, meaning "oil." Hence, it was the garden of the oil press, suggesting that in or near the vineyard stood a stone press for crushing olives and extracting their valued oil.

The olive tree is a deciduous plant, green and flourishing in all seasons, its emerald leaves providing refuge from the desert sun. An ancient Hebrew tradition held that the olive tree was the Tree of Life of scriptural prominence. Like the olive tree, Jesus, the Life of the World, was evergreen, a man for all seasons, a sanctuary from the heat of the world. The wood of the olive tree, prominently used at various places in the construction of Herod's temple at Jerusalem, is singularly distinctive in form and color: alternating bands of dark and light wood are twisted together as if in conflict. The wood's very fibers seem to portray the contest between good and evil that threads through all existence; they may be seen as symbolic of the cosmic struggle that took place in the olive grove at Gethsemane.

The olive press itself is an instrument designed to crush olives by means of a huge circular rock leveraged downward with screws or wooden rods.[2] Before the olives are pressed for their oil, they must be seasoned by storing them for long periods in a solution of salt, vinegar, and purgative herbs; over time this mixture slowly purges them of their bitterness and prepares them as a fruit suitable for eating or for the extraction of oil. Jesus also was prepared and seasoned over a long period, tasting fully of the salt and vinegar of life before he was ripe for the Atonement. Olives, once seasoned, are placed in the olive press to extract their oil. The slow, crushing pressure of the grindstone pulverizes the body and pit of the olive, forcing out the valued oil of culinary pleasure and sacred anointing. Similarly did Jesus the Anointed One endure the crushing weight of the sins of the world until, bruised and broken, he brought forth precious oil of eternal healing. When we use consecrated olive oil in the anointing and healing of the sick today, it is a reminder of his sacrifice in Gethsemane, the garden of the oil press, from whence all blessings flow.

The scriptural accounts of what happened in Gethsemane on the night of the Atonement are sparse, offering only an inkling of the real significance of the event.[3] Matthew records the Savior as saying, "My soul is exceeding sorrowful, even unto death" (Matthew 26:38). Mark uses almost identical language and adds additionally that he became "very heavy" and was "sore amazed" (Mark 14:33–34). Luke's account is shorter than these others, but is the only account that refers to Christ sweating "great drops of blood" (Luke 22:44). Luke also mentions the presence of an angel from heaven "strengthening him" (Luke 22:43). John refers to the crossing of the Savior's entourage from Jerusalem across the brook Cedron (Kidron) to Gethsemane, but gives no account of what happened there, despite his being among the triumvirate of sleep-weary disciples who Christ invited to come deeper into the garden with him.

These accounts by the gospel chroniclers are remarkably brief given that what took place in Gethsemane was the most important event in all of history. The lack of narrative detail stems no doubt in part from the fact that the only witnesses of the event—Peter, James, and John—slept throughout much of their Lord's ordeal. Though Jesus mildly rebuked them for this, asking why they could not watch with him one hour, we must not judge the three disciples too harshly, for their sleep may have served the Father's purpose of ensuring that Christ was truly alone in his hour of supreme trial. Fortunately, we do not have to rely only on the New Testament accounts for understanding of what took place in Gethsemane; we learn more about what happened from modern revelation and from sundry prophecies and portents that appear in the Old Testament and elsewhere.

In this once obscure but now most famous of all gardens, on the eve of Passover, the Lord Jesus Christ took upon himself the sins and sorrows of all mankind, from Adam to the end of the world. He labored under a burden heavier than any other man has ever carried. In the words of James E. Talmage: "Christ's agony in the garden is unfathomable by the finite mind, both as to intensity and cause. . . . He struggled and groaned under a burden such as no other being who has lived on earth might even conceive as possible. It was not physical pain, nor mental anguish alone, that caused Him to suffer such torture as to produce an extrusion of blood from every pore; but a spiritual agony of soul such as only God was capable of experiencing."[4] No mere mortal can atone for the sins of another (Alma 34:10–14), nor could any ordinary mortal have endured what Christ endured and still remained in the flesh. Only the fact that his physical body was partly divine and immortal, as inherited from the Eternal Father, gave him the strength to bear the burden he carried and not perish. But even the immortal half of his nature could not have triumphed had not his human side been steeled and prepared by a lifetime of testing and trial.

Isaiah witnessed in prophetic vision the suffering of Jesus in

Gethsemane: "In all their affliction he was afflicted, and the angel of his presence saved them: in his love and in his pity he redeemed them; and he bare them and carried them all the days of old" (Isaiah 63:9). The "angel of his presence" mentioned here likely refers to the angel that appeared, "strengthening him," as recorded in the book of Luke (22:43). Who was this angel? We know that he could not have been a resurrected being, since no resurrection took place before Christ's own.[5] Instead, he would have been a spirit messenger sent from heaven to succor the Son of Man in his distress. Bruce R. McConkie suggests that the divine messenger was in all probability Michael, best known as the first man, Adam—he who freely brought about the fall of mankind, assisting him who would overcome its effects, the First Adam rendering support to the Second Adam.[6]

Regardless of who he was, we know that this ministering angel did not accompany Christ through his entire ordeal. At least a portion of the Atonement in Gethsemane was borne in utter loneliness. "I have trodden the winepress alone; and of the people there was none with me," declared the voice of Messiah, prefigured by Isaiah (63:3). The winepress mentioned is not an olive press, but rather a large vat used for making wine from grapes. Christ is alluding to the process of trampling the grapes in the vat to prepare them for fermentation, a process that stains the clothing of the tramplers, just as Christ's raiment was stained by the sins of his people. Isaiah foresaw the feelings of Jesus as he trod the winepress alone: "And I looked, and there was none to help; and I wondered that there was none to uphold" (Isaiah 63:5).

The treading of the winepress alone does not refer primarily to Christ's physical isolation in the Garden—to the obliviousness of his sleeping disciples or the departure of the angel of his presence. It pertains rather to the total withdrawal of the spirit of God from his being, that spirit "which is in all things, which giveth life to all things, which is the law by which all things are governed, even the power of God" (D&C 88:13). Without the presence of this spirit, no mortal man could live in the flesh for even an instant, for it is the source of all life and light. Only Jesus Christ, the Great Jehovah, the Self-Existent One (as he was known by the ancient Hebrews) could endure its complete withdrawal and still live—though in such straits of agony as caused him to bleed from every pore. The withdrawal of the Father's spirit was the bitter cup of Gethsemane that Jesus shrank from, yet partook. It was the culminating crucible of the Atonement.

In a revelation to the Prophet Joseph Smith, the Savior spoke of his experience in the Garden:

"For behold, I, God, have suffered these things for all, that they might not suffer if they would repent;

"But if they would not repent they must suffer even as I;

"Which suffering caused myself, even God, the greatest of all, to tremble because of pain, and to bleed at every pore, and to suffer both body and spirit—and would that I might not drink the bitter cup, and shrink—

"Nevertheless, glory be to the Father, and I partook and finished my preparations unto the children of men" (D&C 19:16–19).

Earlier, Christ refers to his sufferings as being "how sore you know not, how exquisite you know not, yea, how hard to bear you know not" (D&C 19:15). He then warns the Prophet and his peers that those who do not repent may face similar suffering of their own: "Wherefore, I command you again to repent, lest I humble you with my almighty power; and that you confess your sins, lest you suffer these punishments of which I have spoken, of which in the smallest, yea, even in the least degree you have tasted at the time I withdrew my Spirit" (D&C 19:20). The Lord's reference to "the time I withdrew my Spirit" is instructive. He is referring to the withdrawal of the Lord's spirit that took place in the Smith household following the loss of the 116 pages of translated manuscript that Joseph had carelessly entrusted to Martin Harris, from whom they were stolen.

The Prophet's mother, Lucy Mack Smith, wrote of the darkness that enveloped the Smith household in the days following the manuscript's loss: "I well remember that day of darkness, both within and without. To us, at least, the heavens seemed clothed with blackness, and the earth shrouded with gloom. I have often said within myself, that if a continual punishment, as severe as that which we experienced on that occasion, were to be inflicted upon the most wicked characters who ever stood upon the footstool of the Almighty—if even their punishment were no greater than that, I should feel to pity their condition."[7] Whatever degree of spiritual darkness fell upon the Smith family at that time, it was only the "least degree" of what Christ experienced in Gethsemane. The withdrawal of the Father's spirit was the immediate and primary cause of the intense agony of body and soul that summoned blood from the Savior's every pore.

The departure of the Spirit left Christ in a wilderness of mind and soul that no other human being has ever experienced. A portent of this can be seen in one of the sacrificial rituals of ancient Israel in which the high priest would take a goat, lay his hands upon its head, and, in figurative ordinance, pronounce upon the head of the animal all of the transgressions and sins of the people. After this, the goat—now a scapegoat, one vicariously bearing the guilt of others—would be led away into the wilderness: "And the goat shall bear upon him all their iniquities *unto a land not inhabited*" (Leviticus 16:22; emphasis added; see also v. 10). In like manner, Christ in Gethsemane was exiled into a spiritual wilderness never before inhabited. No man had ever experienced what he would experience.

At some point in the tribulation of the night, the withdrawal of the Spirit was complete: "And he saw that there was no man, and wondered that there was no intercessor" (Isaiah 59:16). The Lord was alone in a spiritual void, stripped of all sources of solace, cut off from the presence of the Father, bearing in soul and body by virtue of his own strength alone the collective guilt of all mankind. How long the weight of our sins crushed upon him we do not know; how unrelenting his anguish we cannot comprehend. But of that atoning trial, the Savior said, "therefore mine own arm brought salvation unto me; and my fury, it upheld me" (Isaiah 63:5). In the wondrous balance of Heaven's plan, Christ's "own arm"—his divine strength, his virtue, his unyielding love—redeemed us. Neither the angel of his presence, nor even the Eternal Father, came to his aid in that darkest hour. Sheer righteous fury upheld him through the night—the fury of pure love, the fury of determined and mighty righteousness, the fury of the Captain and Bishop of our salvation who refused to yield to despair and perdition, no matter what the cost. Jesus Christ bore the sins and sorrow of the world in what was simply "the greatest single act of love in recorded history."[8]

When Christ delivers up the Kingdom to his Father at the last day, he will declare of the atoning trial: "I have overcome and have trodden the wine-press alone, even the wine-press of the fierceness of the wrath of Almighty God" (D&C 76:107). Though the Great Redeemer was without sin or blemish, he bore the punishment for every iniquity ever committed by humanity—which punishment and divine wrath was manifested in the withdrawal of the Father's spirit, the universal penalty for all sin. He suffered the pain and anguish of every sinner, as though he had committed the sins himself, though he was guiltless. The Innocent One stood in our place, voluntarily bearing the punishment for our transgressions. In Gethsemane, Christ experienced something comparable to spiritual death—being cut off from the presence of God every whit.[9] And just as he would later overcome physical death by means of the Resurrection, he overcame spiritual death by virtue of his triumph that night.

We must not underestimate the price of that victory. On this night that made all days possible, the Savior of the world suffered "the pains of all men, yea, the pains of every living creature, both men, women, and children" (2 Nephi 9:21). He "laid on him the iniquity of us all" (Isaiah 53:6). In the succinct summation of modern revelation: "He descended below all things" (D&C 88:6). The King of Kings descended beneath and overcame every act of iniquity in human history: every murder ever committed, every act of torture and perversion, cruelty and abuse in all their forms, violence, anger, lust, betrayal, deception, theft, envy, and the whole sorry parade of human pride and vanity in their endless forms. Not even a single cross word or impure thought went untouched by the Savior's all-encompassing ransom. From the slightest shadow of sinful desire to the grief and horror of every war ever fought, Christ paid the price for it all.

The love that carried the Redeemer triumphant through Gethsemane was not an abstract or generalized feeling toward mankind as a whole. Rather, it was a personal, deeply felt charity toward each and every individual who ever lived. Isaiah wrote, "when thou shalt make his soul an offering for sin, he shall see his seed" (Isaiah 53:10). The phrase, *when thou shalt make his soul an offering for sin,* apparently refers to the Savior's trial in the Garden, for it was there that he made a ransom or offering for sin; but what is meant by *he shall see his seed?* This seemingly simple phrase offers a possible insight into what transpired at Gethsemane. The prophet Abinadi elaborated on its meaning at length before the court of King Noah:

"Behold, I say unto you, that when his soul has been made an offering for sin he shall see his seed. And now what say ye? And who shall be his seed?

"Behold I say unto you, that whosoever has heard the words of the prophets, yea, all the holy prophets who have prophesied concerning the coming of the Lord—I say unto you, that all those who have hearkened unto their words, and believed that the Lord would redeem his people, and have looked forward to that day for a remission of their sins, I say unto you, that these are his seed, or they are the heirs of the kingdom of God.

"For these are they whose sins he has borne; these are they

for whom he has died, to redeem them from their transgressions. And now, are they not his seed?" (Mosiah 15:10–12).

It would appear that at some point during his ordeal in Gethsemane, the Savior "saw his seed," the myriad individual souls who would accept of his sacrifice and be cleansed by his redeeming power. In seeing them, he knew and loved them; in loving, he suffered for each soul willingly. Gethsemane represented not only the depths of human suffering, but the heights of divine love.

A TRIAL BEFORE THE WORLD: GOD JUDGED BY MEN

After the inexpressible suffering of Christ in the Garden, one might assume that the Great Redeemer had borne enough. But his ordeal was not yet over. Having come off conqueror in a private trial of the soul, the Son of Man now faced a very public trial before the world, a mockery of justice in which the God and Creator of all would be judged and found wanting by profane men. The psalmist had foretold of this trial: "False witnesses did rise up; they laid to my charge things that I knew not" (Psalm 35:11).

Immediately following his ordeal in the olive grove, a clamor was heard, and the party of officers, priests, and Pharisees who would arrest him, led by Judas, was at hand. During the night and day that followed, the Savior of the world was tried and condemned before three separate Jewish tribunals, as well as before the Roman authorities who held ultimate political power in Palestine. Between Gethsemane and Calvary he would suffer, in the words of Frederic Farrar, "a sixfold trial, a quadruple derision, a triple acquittal, a twice repeated condemnation."[10] And, as numerous biblical scholars have pointed out, every one of the various theocratic tribunals that condemned the Savior appears to have been irregular and illegal, both as to procedure and format; in fact, they violated virtually every known tenet of the judicial law of Judaea.[11] In the end, his accusers were compelled to drag him before their Roman overseers whom they professed to detest, but who alone could pronounce a sentence of death upon a man. The only judge of the many Christ faced who seemed to have a problem with this verdict was Pontius Pilate, yet it is he who throughout history has borne the burden of having condemned the Savior to death.

An overarching irony, doubtless of divine design, reigned throughout this day of Christ's trial before men. Here stood the Creator of the world, the great Jehovah, the Law-Giver himself, arraigned before accusers, all of whom owed to him their very existence, each of whose sins—including those of this day—he had borne in suffering. His most ardent impugners to a man proclaimed fealty to the Mosaic law which he himself had instituted from Mount Sinai; now they would cite that law as their basis for convicting him of blasphemy. In Gethsemane he had borne the sins of all mankind; now he was to bear the burden of scornful mockery and the indignation of public humiliation. He must face the world in open trial and overcome it yet again.

Though weakened by his afflictions in the Garden, Jesus bore his day of judgment with supreme composure. His words were few, and more often than not he answered his accusers with granite silence, fulfilling Isaiah's prophecy that "as a sheep before her shearers is dumb, so he openeth not his mouth"

(Isaiah 53:7). His silence reflected neither fear nor recalcitrance. Rather, it was essential to divine law that he remain silent, for any attempt at defense would have legitimized the court before him, and no court on earth could possibly stand in legitimate judgment upon the Creator and God of the world.

His silence thundered loudly during his brief audience with Herod Antipas, tetrarch of Galilee and Perea, the son of Herod the Great who had slaughtered the Babes of Bethlehem. Herod was commonly known as king of the Jews, a title he had not the slightest legal right to hold, but had inherited from his family who had usurped the throne by deceit and violence. It was poetic justice, therefore, that Herod was the only person on record who is known to have seen Christ, the true heir, yet never heard his voice.[12] Unable to elicit words from the Galilean carpenter, Herod and his soldiers contented themselves with mocking Christ and arraying him in "a gorgeous robe" (Luke 23:11), very likely a robe possessed by Herod himself and possibly worn in state on the throne. Where else would so fine a garment have been procured on short notice? By arraying Jesus in kingly raiment, Herod symbolically, if unwittingly, acknowledged him as the true heir to the throne.

The cruelties and indignities suffered by Jesus during the various trials represented a last-ditch effort by Lucifer to cause Christ to stumble. A single misstep—a cross word, an angry outburst, even a moment's indulgence in self-pity or pride—and all was lost. Hence, every possible indignity was heaped upon the Savior: false accusations; blasphemous outbursts; a crown of thorns; the horrible scourging by bone-embedded whips; the mock robe of royalty; the spitting, taunting, and physical blows of the soldiers. The whole pitiable drama was masterminded by Lucifer in the hope that he might yet find a way to nullify the Redeemer's triumph at Gethsemane. Jesus bore it with dignified forbearance. His calm demeanor infuriated his accusers. Nothing he could have said or done would have appeased the hatred of the mob, but the sheer dignity of his presence maddened them beyond all reason. They wanted to humiliate him, pull him down to their level; instead, his kingly bearing chastised them, a quiet rebuke to their homicidal passion.

At every stage of his trial before the Sanhedrin, before Herod, and before Pilate, it seemed that they, not he, were on trial. He was the true judge, not they. The dignified silence with which he met their inquiries, the majesty of his presence, and his manifest courage must have left them all feeling inferior and ashamed, then angry at being ashamed, though unable to help it. The sense that he was judge, not they, no matter how much they tried to humiliate him, galled his accusers, fueling the venom that drove them on. But no matter, for the harder they tried to pull him down, to degrade and abase, the more triumphant his person rose. The whole scene culminated before Pilate in scenes of poignant irony.

The procurator of Judaea, Samaria, and Idumea was the agent of Roman power in Jerusalem, a corrupt and cunning man, indifferent to human life, yet still possessing enough of the spirit of the Lord that he could be touched, even awed, by the presence of Jesus. Arraigned before him was a humble Galilean possessing no social status whatsoever, a man of insignificance in the political hierarchy of the day. While the priestly rulers of the Sanhedrin could feel nothing in their hearts but hatred toward Christ, Pilate's reaction was quite different. Sensing immediately that he was in the presence of an extraordinary man, his questions to the Savior reflected not condemnation, but a genuine desire to understand what accounted for the majesty of his being and the all-penetrating gaze of his eyes.

From the moment he met the Savior, Pilate did everything in his power to forestall the demands for his execution—everything, that is, short of risking mass rioting in the streets. Pilate could not afford a scandal in Jerusalem during the High Feast; his status with his Roman overseers was already shaky due to previous insurrections. But if Pilate lacked courage, he at least retained within him a spark of humanity, something that could not be said of the seething throng before him. His efforts to appease the hatred of the multitude proved futile. Pilate even tried to foist the whole problem off onto Herod, a maneuver that succeeded only in buying a little time. Growing more desperate, Pilate made the traditional offering of the release of one prisoner in recognition of the Passover feast. Thinking he had found a sure gambit, he offered to free either Christ or the hated seditionist and murderer, Barabbas. To his evident surprise, the multitude demanded the release of Barabbas, whose name in Hebrew means *son of the father*. Caught by his own trap, the hapless procurator had no choice but to comply. Hence resulted the irony of Pilate freeing the ultimate embodiment of sin, Barabbas, son of the father, in place of the consummate man of righteousness, Jesus, Son of the Father.

In the end, frustrated and unhappy, the heathen judge washed his hands of all responsibility and turned his prisoner over to the soldiers for scourging, perhaps hoping that this dreaded penalty might yet evoke compassion from his accusers. If this was the motivation, he had badly miscalculated the determination of Christ's enemies.

The scourging itself was in fulfillment of two prophecies of Isaiah: "with his stripes we are healed" (Isaiah 53:5) and "I gave my back to the smiters, and my cheeks to them that plucked off the hair: I hid not my face from shame and spitting" (Isaiah 50:6). A band of Roman soldiers stripped Jesus of his raiment, then whipped him repeatedly with cruel leather thongs in which likely were embedded bits of rock or bone, shredding his back raw and leaving it striped and bloody. Pilate's men placed a plaited crown of thorns upon his head and a reed in his hands for a scepter. Then *for the second time that day* Jesus was arrayed in a majestic robe, this one in the traditional purple color of royalty. Even in derision, again and again, his tormentors inadvertently reaffirmed his kingship.

The prophet Nephi had foreseen his trial in vision: "And the world, because of their iniquity, shall judge him to be a thing of naught; wherefore they scourge him, and he suffereth it; and they smite him, and he suffereth it. Yea, they spit upon him, and he suffereth it, because of his loving kindness and his long-suffering towards the children of men" (1 Nephi 19:9). After all this was accomplished, Pilate brought Jesus before the multitude and pronounced his only real verdict upon him: "Behold, the man!" The declaration rang through the Praetorium with the ring of utter truth. Behold the perfect man, the man who is the embodiment of all manliness, the best and greatest man who ever lived!

Judged by human tribunals and found wanting, Jesus Christ

stood before the world with a stateliness unparalleled in the annals of the human race. His noble but meek demeanor, his serenity in the face of persecution, and the god-like transcendence of his person might have softened the heart of any feeling person. Perhaps counting on such a merciful reaction, Pilate tried three more times to soften the hearts of Christ's accusers and persuade them to drop their demands for his crucifixion. Three times again, his entreaties failed. Devoid of further recourse, Pilate turned his prisoner over to a final ordeal: death by crucifixion.

GOLGOTHA AND THE
TWICE-BORNE CUP

Led forth to his execution, Jesus was forced to carry his cross, or at least the crossbeam thereof, in keeping with the traditions associated with the gruesome rite. Weakened by Gethsemane, by the long night of trials and mockery, and by the near-fatal scourging of the preceding hour, Jesus stumbled and nearly fainted from the weight of the cross. Yet in the bearing of the cross, unlike in most stages of his atoning ordeal, Jesus received assistance from an unexpected source. One Simon, a Cyrenian who was passing through Jerusalem, was apprehended and compelled to bear the cross in Jesus' place. Why Simon was chosen, we do not know—perhaps he protested the inhumane treatment afforded the Savior—but think of the honor that will be his in eternity to have borne, even for a short time, the cross of the Son of Man. Simon's burden is an emblem of discipleship in all eras, for all who would serve God must in some measure bear the cross of Christ, bending and sacrificing, even in the face of adversity, if they are to be found at his right side in the Judgment Day. In allowing Simon to bear his cross, Jesus also taught us to receive service willingly, to let others bear our burdens with us as we traverse through life.

The hour of crucifixion had arrived. Jesus had prophesied of the manner of his death: "And I, if I be lifted up from the earth, will draw all men unto me" (John 12:32). The Passover offering transpired at Golgotha, "place of the skull," so named, perhaps, either because the hillock was itself shaped like a skull, as seen from above, or because the limestone formations around the base of the hill appeared very much in form like an actual human skull. Golgotha likely lay just to the north of what is today the Damascus Gate. The execution thus occurred outside the city wall, as the law required. The place of crucifixion also fulfilled a prophetic type: it occurred on the northern rim of the raised plateau of Jerusalem, just as blood offerings on the altars of Israel always had taken place on the north side of the temple altars (Leviticus 1:11).[13]

The events of the Crucifixion, including the seven pronouncements of Christ upon the cross, were prefigured in remarkable detail in many of the Messianic psalms of David, particularly the twenty-second Psalm, which in its entirety is a prophetic recounting of the circumstances of the Savior's execution. Other Old Testament prophecies also reveal much of what we know of those dark hours during which transpired the Passover sacrifice toward which all other Passover sacrifices had pointed for centuries past.

For dogs have compassed me: the assembly of the wicked have inclosed me: they pierced my hands and my feet—Psalm 22:16

> *And I will fasten him as a nail in a sure place*—Isaiah 22:23[14]

These prophecies of David and Isaiah were now literally fulfilled, as Roman soldiers nailed Jesus of Nazareth to a cross and lifted him up in midst of the assembly of the wicked. We know from the testimony of the risen Lord that nails were driven in his hands and feet (Luke 24:40; 3 Nephi 11:14). The best available archaeological evidence suggests that nails also "pierced the forearms (passing between the radius and the ulna) and held them to the cross."[15] There is no need to dwell further here on the physical details of the Crucifixion. The gruesome intricacies of this peculiarly Roman form of punishment have been described in detail in other works.[16] Suffice it to say that crucifixion was widely regarded as the most horrible form of death that could be inflicted on any person. Far better to be burned at the stake or impaled, and thus die a swift death, than suffer the slow, excruciating torment of crucifixion. In the apex of the Roman Empire, when this form of execution was common, thousands, perhaps even tens of thousands, suffered this fate. In this sense, Christ's physical pains upon the cross were not without precedence. But in another sense his suffering was entirely unique, for throughout his hours on the cross he possessed the power to free himself from the torture at any moment. He who had withered the fig tree could surely have withered the cross or indeed any or all of his mockers and executioners. What pains he bore, he bore freely and willingly. The strength of will needed to endure such agonizing torment, when release stood but a word's command away, is incomprehensible to mortal minds.

At the end of the twenty-second chapter of Isaiah, the Lord

God speaks of "my servant" (Christ) as the heir to David's throne, promising to clothe him with a royal robe and give him the keys of government over Judah. In reference to the Crucifixion, he says, "I will fasten him as a nail in a sure place" (Isaiah 22:23). There follows a poignant allegory of the Atonement: "And they shall hang upon him all the glory of his father's house, the offspring and the issue, all vessels of small quantity, from the vessels of cups, even to all the vessels of flagons" (v. 24). All vessels in the Father's house—every one of God's children—hang upon the Savior, even as he hung upon the cross. It is a vision of the utter dependence of every human creature, both great and small, on the grace of the Atonement.

Shew me a token for good; that they which hate me may see it, and be ashamed—Psalm 86:17[17]

When the Roman soldiers who carried out Christ's execution lifted up the cross on which he was nailed, the astonished onlookers saw a title, probably a wooden placard, nailed above the Savior's head: JESUS OF NAZARETH THE KING OF THE JEWS, written in Hebrew and Greek and Latin, so as to insure that no one would fail to understand it. Pilate, the heathen procurator, was determined to make one last statement of his real opinion of Christ, a final, ringing affirmation of his royal station, and so he had ordered the sign to be made. Enraged and ashamed of what it implied, the Jewish leaders present at the Crucifixion dispatched a deputation to Pilate demanding that the offensive title be removed or at least be changed: "Write not, The King of the Jews; but that he said, I am King of the Jews" (John 19:21). Pilate held his ground, answering simply, "What I have written I have written" (John

19:22). He refused all further entreaty. Pilate's obduracy made certain that all who witnessed Christ's execution would plainly read the true status of the condemned Galilean: he was their appointed King, as he would remain their King forever.

> *But I am a worm, and no man; a reproach of men, and despised of the people. All they that see me laugh me to scorn: they shoot out the lip, they shake the head, saying, He trusted on the Lord that he would deliver him: let him deliver him, seeing he delighted in him*—Psalm 22:6–8

> *But in mine adversity they rejoiced. . . . With hypocritical mockers in feasts, they gnashed upon me with their teeth*—Psalm 35:15–16

The scorn and mockery flung at Christ during the inquisitions of the preceding day continued during the long hours on the cross. Lucifer would yield no ground in his determination to bruise the heel of the unblemished lamb. By means of the taunting sneers of worldly minions, he tormented Christ to the last. Again and again the raging spectators derided his claim to be the Son of God, their words barbed with the same accusatory *if* that Lucifer had thrown at him during his temptations in the wilderness: "*If* thou be the Son of God, come down from the cross" (Matthew 27:40; emphasis added). Or in different words: "Let Christ the King of Israel descend now from the cross, that we may see and believe" (Mark 15:32). Lucifer's snare was not aimed at causing Christ to doubt his mission; that would have been impossible, for he knew with absolute certainty that he was the Son of God and the chosen Messiah. Satan's plan was more devious—he wanted to tempt Christ to *prove* that he was the Son of God, to overawe his revilers with some manifestation of blinding power. Had Jesus done so, his vindication would have been short-lived, and Satan would have come off the ultimate victor. Only by Christ's forswearing the divine power within him and submitting humbly to the depredations of his crucifiers could the Atonement be consummated.

I have spread out my hands all the day unto a rebellious people—Isaiah 65:2

These words from Isaiah have been interpreted as prophetic of the Savior's stance during the Crucifixion, when his arms and hands were spread out on the cross in symbolic embrace of the city of Jerusalem, which city he cherished beyond words. Earlier he had declared, "O Jerusalem, Jerusalem . . . how often would I have gathered thy children together, even as a hen gathereth her chickens under her wings, and ye would not!" (Matthew 23:37). But his love was not for the Holy City alone, or even for its inhabitants. Though his earthly mission was to the Jewish people, the remnant of Israel, his love was universal, embracing the whole human race. No more eloquent expression of that love is found than in the Lord's first pronouncement from the cross: "Father, forgive them; for they know not what they do" (Luke 23:34). Love was his watchword and forgiveness his song, even in the agony of the cross.

The Lord's expression of mercy was directed primarily to the Roman soldiers carrying out the execution under command of their superiors. They truly had no conception of what they did. The case of the religious leaders who masterminded his death is more complex. They had shed innocent blood, indeed the most perfectly innocent blood ever shed; they had crucified the God of heaven and earth in a fury of blind envy and hatred.

But we ought not to place limits on the scope of the Lord's Atonement. His words hinted also of a grace and eventual pardon—conditional upon repentance—that might be granted to the priests, scribes, and officials of the Sanhedrin who had pursued him to his death. For all their hypocrisy and hardness of heart, they too were children of God, who had no real comprehension of how awful was their crime. Jesus was also their Redeemer; through him, and only through him, might they have hope of pardon. "The very foes who slay thee have access to thy grace."[18]

They part my garments among them, and cast lots upon my vesture—Psalm 22:18

The four Roman soldiers responsible for carrying out the crucifixion evidently had claim on the clothing and immediate property of the condemned. That part of Christ's garments which they could share, they divided into four parts; his coat, which would have been ruined by dividing it, they chose to keep in one piece and cast lots to determine who should have it. Thus were the garments sullied of him who alone has power to make our own garments clean; the garments divided of him who alone can make us whole.

For he hath not despised nor abhorred the affliction of the afflicted; neither hath he hid his face from him; but when he cried unto him, he heard—Psalm 22:24

Even as he hung in agony on the cross, Jesus was mindful of "the affliction of the afflicted," the two convicted thieves who were on either side of him. Even as he had taken upon himself the sins of the world, in his death "he was numbered with the transgressors" (Isaiah 53:12). One of them railed against him, joining the mob in taunting, "If thou be Christ, save thyself and us" (Luke 23:39). But the other criminal rebuked the mocker, defending Christ as one who had done no wrong. Whether or not this condemned man actually knew anything of Christ, we do not know. But evidently he could see enough of his regal composure on the cross and godly look in his eyes to recognize a king when he saw one. "Lord, remember me when thou comest into thy kingdom" (Luke 23:42). Jesus answered him in the second recorded statement made from the cross: "Verily I say unto thee, To day shalt thou be with me in paradise" (Luke 23:43).

I behaved myself as though he had been my friend or brother: I bowed down heavily, as one that mourneth for his mother—Psalm 35:14

Among the few followers of Christ who dared to attend his execution were three women, all named Mary—the mother of Jesus; his mother's sister, the wife of Cleopas; and Mary Magdalene. Only one of the apostles, beloved John, was courageous enough to be present. Despite the weight of the world that lay upon him, Jesus was especially mindful of his mother, Mary. Gazing with tenderness upon the Jewish woman who had borne and raised him, he said to her, "Woman, behold thy son!" (John 19:26). The phrase thus uttered may have had a double meaning. While Christ was clearly directing his mother to John as an adopted son and provider, his words might just as easily have referred to himself: Woman, behold thy son, he whose birth the angels proclaimed, he who turned the water into wine at thy request; behold thy son, now raised upon a cross.

Then Jesus looked upon John and said, "Behold thy

mother!" (John 19:27). Having risked his life to witness his Master's execution, John received the singular honor of caring for the mother of Jesus through the remainder of her life. How long that stewardship lasted and what sacrifices it entailed, we do not know; it is a story whose telling awaits the future. But in designating John as the adopted son and guardian of his mother, Jesus was also acknowledging the special relationship that existed between him and the beloved disciple: "as though he had been my friend or brother" (Psalm 35:14).

> My God, my God, why hast thou forsaken me? why art thou so far from helping me, and from the words of my roaring?—Psalm 22:1

All told, the Savior made seven recorded pronouncements from the cross. The most poignant and haunting of these was the fourth: "*Eloi, Eloi, lama sabachthani?*" (Mark 15:34). After a sleepless night of accusations and trials; after a day of shuttling between accusers; after scourging and mockery and the torment of crucifixion; after all that, Christ confronted the dark anguish of the Garden yet again. The spirit of God withdrew entirely from him and the agony of Gethsemane recurred in an unexpected and sorrow-ridden reprise: "My God, my God, why hast thou forsaken me?" At the moment of his greatest humiliation before men, when the world had abandoned him and his disciples fled, the Father's spirit retreated also, causing the Creator of the world to cry out in desperation.

Some of the spectators, hearing the Hebrew word "Eloi," thought that Jesus was calling for the prophet Elias. Others likely presumed, as have many biblical scholars, that he was quoting the first line of Psalm 22. In fact, he was not quoting the psalm, but fulfilling it. In the words of James Talmage:

"What mind of man can fathom the significance of that awful cry? It seems, that in addition to the fearful suffering incident to crucifixion, the agony of Gethsemane had recurred, intensified beyond human power to endure. . . . That the supreme sacrifice of the Son might be consummated in all its fulness, the Father seems to have withdrawn the support of His immediate Presence, leaving to the Savior of men the glory of complete victory over the forces of sin and death."[19]

The bitter cup that Christ had shrunk to drink at Gethsemane, but partook out of obedience to the Father, he now tasted once more in full measure. To the physical torment of crucifixion was added the incomprehensible weight he had borne in the olive grove. Once again, Jesus was cut off from every source of solace, including the presence of his Father. And to the inexpressible pain of that twice-borne cup was added the scorn and derision of Jerusalem's masses. Thus, in the culminating moments of his life, the Redeemer experienced the combined burden of all the trials he had faced in the preceding two days: the physical torture of crucifixion; the spiritual anguish caused by the withdrawal of the Father's spirit; the ordeal of rejection and mockery by the people he loved so much. The pressure that bore down upon his soul in these last moments of life is beyond all comprehension. The end was near, but before it came the Savior was to make three more statements, each of great significance, though the first two consisted of only five words combined.

My strength is dried up like a potsherd; and my tongue cleaveth to my jaws; and thou hast brought me into the dust of death—Psalm 22:15

"I thirst," (John 19:28) was his next cry. Horrible, ravenous, unquenchable thirst was one of the most dreaded symptoms of crucifixion. Dehydrated from loss of blood and from the shock of mind-numbing pains, the victims of crucifixion were driven nearly mad from thirst. No doubt the Savior suffered the same excruciating want. It may seem curious that after all he had borne, Christ would make a statement of physical need, but there is an important lesson and a deeper meaning contained in his words. Earlier, when offered a narcotic draught to relieve his pain, the Savior had refused. But now, on the very brink of his death, he accepted the relief of a small portion of vinegar soaked in a sponge and raised with a hyssop to his mouth: "In my thirst they gave me vinegar to drink" (Psalm 69:21). When every imaginable suffering had been borne, and the world in its fullness conquered, Christ accepted relief from his fellow-man, teaching again that all true service entails a willingness to be served.

Yet his statement of thirst may not have been only an expression of physical want. The Master thirsted for drink, yes, but he thirsted also for the completion of the Atonement, for the one eternal victory that spelled salvation for his people. He thirsted for their redemption, for their reconciliation with the Father, for the eternal life that only he could bring them. The physical thirst tormenting him was a reflection of a far deeper spiritual thirst that had been with him his whole life. This was the Nazarene who had called himself "Living Water" and offered to give men drink that they might never thirst; this was the Great Jehovah whose very voice was as the sound of rushing waters. On the cross, he endured the thirst of death so that he might quench with eternal refreshment the souls of all who would receive him.

I am poured out like water, and all my bones are out of joint: my heart is like wax; it is melted in the midst of my bowels—Psalm 22:14

Reproach hath broken my heart; and I am full of heaviness: and I looked for some to take pity, but there was none; and for comforters, but I found none—Psalm 69:20

We have reason to believe that the cause of Christ's death was a broken heart. The immediate physical cause of death was likely a cardiac rupture, a medical phenomenon that would have poured congealed blood, water, and serum into the pericardium cavity of his chest, accounting for the flow of fluid that issued forth when the Roman soldier pierced his side with the sword.[20] It is possible that the sword actually pierced in or near his heart, creating the channel through which the blood and water poured out. But the Master's heart not only ruptured physically, it was broken in a higher, spiritual sense—out of sheer sorrow for the wickedness of a people who would crucify their God, for the sin and iniquity of the human race, for the inherent tragedy of a fallen world. His mother, Mary, watching the final incontestable evidence of his passing, must have experienced a wave of intense grief, foreshadowed in the words of Simeon at the temple thirty-three years earlier: "Yea, a sword shall pierce through thy own soul also" (Luke 2:35).

Speaking in first person, as though he were the Lord, the psalmist in two prophetic passages describes the Savior's condition in the final moments before his death: "I am full of heaviness" and "My heart is like wax; it is melted in the midst of my bowels" (Psalms 69:20; 22:14). Because he had the power to give up his life when he chose, it appears that Jesus lingered for a time after his heart had ruptured, filling him with heaviness like wax. Utterly sacrificed and totally used up, Immanuel had won the victory over sin and death. His heart broken, his body torn and bruised, he yet found the strength to proclaim in a voice of triumph that his redeeming mission was fulfilled: "It is finished" (John 19:30).

> *He shall see of the travail of his soul, and shall be satisfied*—Isaiah 53:11

It would appear that the spirit of God, withdrawn from the Savior for a time, had returned, confirming that his sacrifice was accepted of the Father and the Atonement was fully consummated. Whatever agonies Jesus suffered on the cross, he knew in the final moments of his life the joy of ultimate victory. Satisfied that his work on earth was done, he spoke his last reverent words, "Father, into thy hands I commend my spirit" (Luke 23:46), and the Anointed One departed the realm of tears.

As darkness, storm, and earthquake descended upon Jerusalem, few if any would have fathomed the meaning of his parting cry of triumph, but in realms on high, angelic hosts surely were weeping with joy and rejoicing in song. Jesus' agony was over! Love's redeeming work was done! Christ had paid the ransom's price.

TRIUMPH OF TRIUMPHS

At the moment of the Redeemer's death, the veil of the temple in Jerusalem was "rent in twain" (Mark 15:38), torn down the middle in two halves, exposing the inner sanctum of the Holy of Holies to view. This was not an act of divine retribution, as some have suggested, but rather a sacred token of the consummation of the Atonement.

The Holy of Holies was the most sacred enclave of the Temple, the sanctuary where originally had been kept the ark of the covenant and the mercy seat. Only one man, the high priest, was allowed to enter this inner sanctum, and then but once a year on the Day of Atonement and only after elaborate ritual purification—for to enter the Holy of Holies was to enter the place where God had manifested himself to ancient Israel in past times and where he might again manifest himself. Symbolically, the purified high priest stood as proxy for the sinless Messiah, who alone was worthy to enter the presence of God. Until the Atonement was accomplished, no mortal soul could enter back into the presence of the Eternal Father. But at the moment of Christ's passing, the demands of justice were paid, the power of death defeated, and the way open for every penitent soul to pass through the veil into royal courts on high. The rending of the veil proclaimed to the world that Christ had opened the gate of heaven and mankind was no longer shut out from the presence of God.

The twenty-second Psalm foretells Christ's victory in these words: "All they that go down to the dust shall bow before him: and none can keep alive his own soul. A seed shall serve him; it shall be accounted to the Lord for a generation. They shall come, and shall declare his righteousness unto a people that shall be born, *that he hath done this*" (vv. 29–31; emphasis added). Jesus of Nazareth had done what he came to do. Immediately after this closing declaration of the twenty-second Psalm, there follows the most eloquent anthem of peace ever penned:

The Lord is my shepherd;
I shall not want.
He maketh me to lie down in green pastures:
He leadeth me beside the still waters . . .
Yea, though I walk through the valley of the shadow of death,
I will fear no evil: for thou art with me;
Thy rod and thy staff they comfort me.

The Good Shepherd came to ransom his life for the sheep.
All who accept of that ransom and come unto him will find
rest in his fold and peace to their souls.

CHAPTER SIX

KEEPER OF THE GATE

In her haunting short story, "Revelation," the American author Flannery O'Connor relates a modern-day parable of the Judgment Day. It is a story of one Mrs. Turpin, a Southern woman of modest wealth and genteel lineage. Mrs. Turpin is a good Christian woman who sincerely seeks to help her neighbors, even those she considers to be poor blacks and "white trash." Though privately looking down on such people, she treats them politely on the surface. Living in the days before the civil rights movement, Mrs. Turpin has some fairly strong racial and class prejudices: "Mrs. Turpin occupied herself at night naming the classes of people. On the bottom of the heap were most colored people . . . then next to them—not above, just away from—were the white-trash; then above them were the home-owners, and above them the home-and-land owners, to which she and Claud belonged. Above she and Claud were people with a lot of money and much bigger houses and much more land."[1] While sitting in a doctor's waiting room one day, Mrs. Turpin is attacked by a mentally disturbed young woman who has overheard her conversation laced with subtle disdain for these presumably lower classes. Without warning, the young woman flings a book at Mrs. Turpin and tries to choke her, before being pulled off and dispatched to a mental hospital. But before being dragged away, the woman screams at Mrs. Turpin, denouncing her as a creature from hell.

Mrs. Turpin is devastated by the experience. She goes home to the family farm deeply troubled, unable to shake the notion that God had sent her a message through the young lady. Growing increasingly agitated, she cries out a prayer of anger and despair to the darkening sky: "What do you send me a message like that for?" she cries. "It's no trash around here, black or white, that I haven't given to. And break my back to the bone every day working. And do for the church."[2] Moments later, Mrs. Turpin has the revelation alluded to in the title of the story. A purple streak suspended above the setting sun suddenly appears to her as a bridge reaching upward from earth to heaven:

> Upon it a vast horde of souls were rumbling toward heaven. There were whole companies of white-trash, clean for the first time in their lives, and bands of black[s] . . . in white robes, and battalions of freaks and lunatics shouting and clapping and leaping like frogs. And bringing up the end of the procession was a tribe of people she recognized at once [as her own]. . . . They were marching behind the others with great dignity, accountable as they had always been for good order and common sense and respectable behavior. They alone were on key. Yet she could see by their shocked and altered faces that even their virtues were being burned away.[3]

The vision closes with Mrs. Turpin hearing voices crying hallelujah in the starry skies.

Keen insights are contained in O'Connor's stark allegory of the Judgment Day. Much of what is regarded as good and respectable will be revealed at that day as superficial or hypocritical. The pecking order of the world will be shaken up, even turned upside down, by the judgments of heaven. The mentally impaired and ill, the downtrodden and lowly of the earth, children who died in their infancy and made no mark on the world—these shall shine forth in the kingdom of heaven, while many of the privileged and exalted of the earth will be brought low. There will be a great upheaval of human expectations and hopes, as "many that are first shall be last; and the last shall be first" (Matthew 19:30).

In anticipation of that day, no person should assume that his or her virtues and good works will suffice to earn entrance to the kingdom of heaven. As Mrs. Turpin learned of the respectable people with whom she associated, "even their virtues were being burned away," as the purifying fire of Heaven's all-knowing judgment mocked every pretense and exposed every hidden weakness, even those thought to be strengths in the eyes of their possessors. At that day, all of God's children shall come to know just how dependent their salvation is upon the Atonement and grace of the Redeemer, how small are human virtues and deeds, and how great are the shortcomings of even the best.

The thought of judgment makes most human beings feel uncomfortable, but judgment is an inescapable fact of life, both in this world and in the hereafter. The concept of judgment figures prominently throughout the scriptures. Derivatives of the word *judge* (including judged, judges, and judgment) appear 1,853 times in holy writ. The only words that appear more often are those pertaining to God and the Godhead. Other doctrinal terms, such as love, salvation, faith, grace, repentance, and their related forms, have a few hundred entries each. Only the word *commandment* and its various derivatives come even close to the word *judgment* in frequency. Of course, the frequency of words alone does not establish their relative importance in gospel doctrine; nevertheless, the prominence of the theme of judgment in the scriptures is one evidence of how important that final day shall be. The Scottish theologian William Barclay has observed that the great majority of Christ's parables are allegories or teachings about the Last Judgment.[4] These include the parables of the wheat and the tares, the unforgiving debtor, the wedding feast, the draw net, the talents, the rich fool, the barren fig tree, the Pharisee and the publican, the sheep and the goats, the rich man and Lazarus, the unjust judge, the laborers in the vineyard, the prodigal son, and the ten virgins.[5] Many of the prominent Book of Mormon discourses on the plan of salvation—2 Nephi 9; Mosiah 3; Alma 5; Alma 42—also center in substantial measure around the day of judgment.

Judgment is an essential component of a divinely governed universe. Without it, there would be no accountability; and without accountability, no right or wrong. And without judgment, without right and wrong, as Nephi taught, there would be no opposition in all things, no sorrow or joy, no life or death, no purpose or meaning to existence (2 Nephi 2:10–13). Every human society, state, kingdom, or civilization that ever existed has had laws and judges. None could have survived without such, for anarchy would result if the principle of judgment, even flawed and imperfect human judgment, was swept away. Yet while human courts may err and commit travesties of justice, the heavenly court that awaits us is a court of perfect mercy and justice. The judge of that tribunal is none other than Jesus Christ himself.

THE KING OF KINGS
AS THE ETERNAL JUDGE

The authority of Christ as Judge of the world follows naturally from his preeminent status as King of Kings. Throughout all ages, in all quarters of the globe, the monarchs of the earth have served as the highest judges of their people. Kingship and judgeship are everywhere and always inextricably linked. Though almost every kingdom in history has had its lesser magistrates and judges, all ultimate appeals went to the king, who as law-giver and sovereign had the final say in all judiciary matters. In this regard, monarchies distinguish themselves from modern representative governments in that the executive and judicial powers are always one in a monarchy, though normally separate in a republic or democracy. The monarchical pattern also holds true in the kingdom of heaven, where Immanuel is both King and final judge of all. At the Judgment Day no appeal to a higher sovereign will be possible, not even the Eternal Father, "For the Father judgeth no man, but hath committed all judgment unto the Son" (John 5:22).[6]

As in earthly kingdoms, we know that certain lesser magistrates will play a role at the final judgment, the highest among their ranks being the twelve apostles who served with Christ in Jerusalem.[7] The Savior promised his apostles: "And I appoint unto you a kingdom, as my Father hath appointed unto me; that ye may eat and drink at my table in my

kingdom, and sit on thrones judging the twelve tribes of Israel"
(Luke 22:29–30). The Book of Mormon teaches that the
twelve apostles chosen by Christ from among the Nephites in
Bountiful will also play a role in judging their people, but it
will be a subordinate role to the twelve in Jerusalem.[8] Nephi
and Moroni each state that they will stand at the judgment
seat to testify against those who reject their words (2 Nephi
33:11; Moroni 10:27). It is very likely that other prophets and
priesthood leaders will play lesser roles in the preliminary judgment of their people, prior to the final judgment by the
Savior.[9] But one thing is certain: the culmination of the judgment for every child of God will take place before the tribunal
bar of the Great Jehovah, Jesus Christ himself. As the Apostle
Paul taught, "For we must all appear before the judgment seat
of Christ; that every one may receive . . . according to that he
hath done, whether it be good or bad" (2 Corinthians 5:10).[10]

Every human being who ever lived will stand individually
before the King to account for his life and receive the rightful
measure of justice and grace at his hand: "O then, my beloved
brethren, come unto the Lord, the Holy One. Remember that
his paths are righteous. Behold, the way for man is narrow, but
it lieth in a straight course before him, and *the keeper of the gate
is the Holy One of Israel; and he employeth no servant there;* and
there is none other way save it be by the gate; for he cannot
be deceived, for the Lord God is his name" (2 Nephi 9:41;
emphasis added). None can evade this interview. None will
enter the Kingdom of Heaven without passing by the
Anointed One of Nazareth. He is the Door, the Keeper of the
Gate.

WHY JESUS CHRIST ALONE
CAN BE A PERFECT JUDGE

The supernal qualifications of Christ to serve as our Eternal Judge are best revealed when we compare his qualifications with those of any merely mortal magistrate. Let us imagine that at the Judgment Day, our eternal destiny were to be decided by an ordinary mortal, someone who did not know us, but who had the reputation of being an impartial judge. We might immediately raise several valid objections to such an arrangement.

"Who are you to judge me?" would be the first objection. "You are a flawed human being, just as I am. By what right do you, in all your imperfection, presume to judge me?"

Though such a protest might fairly be raised against any human judge, no such objection can be made to the judgment of the Son of Man, for Jesus Christ was and is perfect, his very flawlessness constituting his most obvious qualification to stand as our Judge. He is on a higher plane than any mortal, a man who lived without sin and never succumbed to temptation; he is neither our equal nor our peer but a manifestly superior being. Indeed, he is God and will judge as no man possibly can.

To continue this line of thought, if an ordinary human being were to judge us, we might further object: "You have not stood in my shoes. You have no conception of the pain and sorrow I have suffered, the circumstances of my upbringing, the trials and setbacks of my life, nor do you understand in any degree the temptations I have faced. How, then, can you presume to judge me?"

Here again, such an objection, though valid when applied

to one of our peers, cannot apply to the judgment of the Master. For he who overcame the world intimately knows our sorrows, has plumbed the depths of pain, and was himself "tempted in all points," that he might qualify as a perfect, all-understanding, and all-knowing judge. This is surely one reason why the Father committed judgment into his hands—it was only right that the people of this earth be judged by one who had lived on the earth. Christ's divine omniscience further means that at the Judgment Day he will know every intimate detail of our lives, including all the obstacles and extenuating circumstances we faced, and he will take every circumstance into account, weighed in the balance of perfect love.

To any mortal judge, yet another objection might be raised: "You claim to be a compassionate judge, yet you are an ordinary man, even as I am. How can I possibly trust that your love is so perfect that you would not even in the least degree judge me too harshly or withhold any blessing I might merit?"

The compassion of even the best of men might be questioned if eternity hung in the balance. But there will not be the slightest cause to question the love or mercy of the Savior at the Judgment; his perfect love was proven in Gethsemane and on Calvary when he took upon himself the sins and iniquities of the human race, suffering "the pains of all men, yea, the pains of every living creature, both men, women, and children, who belong to the family of Adam" (2 Nephi 9:21).

It is here, in fact, that the contrast between Christ and any mortal judge becomes so stark. In Victor Hugo's novel, *Les Misérables*, a poor Frenchman named Jean Valjean is condemned to prison for stealing a loaf of bread to feed his sister's family.[11] Imagine now when Jean Valjean was brought before the magistrate to be sentenced that the following dialogue had ensued:

> *Judge:* "Are you guilty of the crime for which you are charged? Did you steal the loaf of bread?"
>
> *Jean Valjean:* "I did."
>
> *Judge:* "Then the law requires that I sentence you to three years in prison. I have no discretion in this matter. But first, tell me how you feel about this crime."
>
> *Jean Valjean:* "In the beginning, I thought I was justified. But I now realize that the law ought not to have been broken, despite our poverty. I feel intense guilt and sorrow for my decision, which has brought greater pain on my sister and her children than any relief the bread might have provided. I know it was wrong and regret it with all my heart. I will not do it again. Your honor, I have repaid the bakery for the stolen loaf and offered my most abject apology."
>
> *Judge:* "Your penitence is obviously sincere, and you have made every possible restitution. Mercy would call for your pardon and release, but justice demands that a penalty be paid, and this court cannot mock justice. There is only one way I can be compassionate toward you and still render a just verdict. To satisfy the demands of the law, *I will serve your sentence for you.*"

Such a scenario would seem utterly fantastic if played out in any earthly tribunal, and it is virtually certain that nothing like that last sentence has ever been uttered in any human court. Yet in figurative form, it captures the surpassing love that will reign at the Judgment. Having personally paid the penalty for our sins, having "served our sentence for us," Jesus Christ will stand as a judge of incontestable kindness, freely forgiving all who come to him in lowliness of heart. Knowing of his suffering on our behalf, how will anyone question the mercy of his judgment? Every knee will bow and every tongue confess that he is the rightful judge of all God's children.

BY WHAT CRITERIA
WILL MEN BE JUDGED?

Because we must all stand individually before the King to be judged, it is imperative that we understand the terms and conditions of that judgment. We would not enroll in a high school or university course without knowing the requirements of success and the standards of grading; why then would we go through life without knowing by what criteria Christ shall judge us?

The fourth Article of Faith lays out the fundamental requirements of salvation in the celestial kingdom. Every person desiring entrance into that kingdom must first exercise faith in the Lord Jesus Christ, the only "name given under heaven whereby man can be saved in the kingdom of God" (2 Nephi 31:21). Second, he or she must repent of sin, for "no unclean thing can enter into his kingdom" (3 Nephi 27:19). Third, the candidate must have been baptized by immersion by the proper priesthood authority, baptism being an eternal covenant referred to in the scriptures as the "gate" or "way" into the kingdom (2 Nephi 31:17–18). This ordinance must take place in the flesh, either in person or by proxy. Fourth, the aspiring entrant must receive the gift of the Holy Ghost, which has the power to sanctify and cleanse from sin (3 Nephi 27:20). The Holy Ghost will teach, testify, and guide in every path of righteousness, manifesting "all things what ye should do" (2 Nephi 32:5). Finally, as many other passages of scripture teach, an individual must remain true to his testimony and covenants throughout mortality and "endure to the end," or his efforts will be in vain (2 Nephi 31:16).

These are the essential requirements of salvation, the irreducible prerequisites for entry into the celestial kingdom. All persons who would enter into the *highest* degree of glory in that kingdom must additionally receive the higher ordinances of exaltation found only in the holy temple of God, including the new and everlasting covenant of marriage. Since the gift of exaltation is received only in the highest degree of glory, the temple and its ordinances embody the highest aspirations of every true disciple of Christ.

While this list of statutory prerequisites is absolutely mandatory, the Judgment will entail more than satisfying a series of formal requirements. Baptism without repentance is an empty ritual. Faith without works is dead. Confirmation does not guarantee that the confirmed member will actually receive the Holy Ghost and heed its promptings. The scriptures make clear that we will be judged not only by the letter of the celestial law, but also by the spiritual substance of our lives. We will be held accountable for every deed, word, and thought. Even the most righteous must make an accounting of his life's choices before the Savior. In Christ's own words, "I say unto you, That every idle word that men shall speak, they shall give account thereof in the day of judgment" (Matthew 12:36).

There are nearly thirty scriptural references to men being "judged by their works" at the last day. John the Revelator, for instance, states unequivocally that men will be judged "according to their works" (Revelation 20:12–13). Alma taught that men will be judged both by their works and by the desires of their hearts: "And it is requisite with the justice of God that men should be judged according to their works; and if their works were good in this life, and the desires of their hearts were good, that they should also, at the last day, be restored unto that which is good" (Alma 41:3). The desires of the heart are crucial. Since good works are sometimes done grudgingly, for hypocritical motives, or for outward show, the mere fact of them proves nothing; they are acceptable before God only when they stem from pure intent. Mere professions of faith are also meaningless: "Not every one that saith unto me, Lord, Lord, shall enter into the kingdom of heaven; but he that doeth the will of my Father which is in heaven" (Matthew 7:21).

The doctrine that men will be *judged* by their works is not the same as the notion that men are *saved* by their works. Good works alone can never bring about salvation absent the Atonement of Christ, for good works do not compensate for sins commited. Yet righteous desires are nonetheless manifested in good works, both being reflections of the inner heart. Because none is perfect and none will be able to claim that all his works and desires were good, a great deal will ride on the simple word, "repentance." To repent is to experience a change of heart and come unto Christ with a broken heart and a contrite spirit, for "unto none else can the ends of the law be answered" (2 Nephi 2:7). Only when our hearts are freely given to the Savior can that spiritual cleansing take place that makes possible entry into God's kingdom.

Because every person will be accountable for every act of agency, we need to ask by what criteria our works, words, desires, and thoughts will be judged. We need to know what we must repent of, what we must forsake, what will count, and what will not.

Let us begin with what will *not* count at the Day of Judgment.

Our property and wealth will count as naught. "For what is property unto me? saith the Lord" (D&C 117:4). Jesus taught his disciples that the treasures of the earth were of no enduring worth and admonished them to forsake their pursuit, for "Ye cannot serve God and mammon" (Matthew 6:24). He counseled the rich young man to sell all that he had and give it to the poor, declaring that "it is easier for a camel to go through the eye of a needle, than for a rich man to enter into the kingdom of God" (Mark 10:25). And in modern revelation we read: "Wo unto you rich men, that will not give your substance to the poor, for your riches will canker your souls; and this shall be your lamentation in the [Day of Judgment]: . . . The harvest is past, the summer is ended, and my soul is not saved!" (D&C 56:16). In a quite literal sense, wealth *cannot* count at the Last Judgment, for as Paul wrote Timothy: "We brought nothing into this world, and it is certain we can carry nothing out" (1 Timothy 6:7). Rich and poor will stand on equal ground at the bar of Christ, both owning nothing at all.

Our honors, titles, and temporal achievements will count as naught. The praise, preferments, and high offices of the world, on which we tend to place great value, will be of no more worth than money at the judgment bar. "I receive not honour from men," said the Savior, adding the pointed question: "How can ye believe, which receive honour one of another, and seek not the honour that cometh from God only?" (John 5:41, 44). Christ reproached the scribes and Pharisees for their love of high station and worldly acclaim: "But all their works they do for to be seen of men: they . . . love the uppermost rooms at feasts, and the chief seats in the synagogues, and greetings in the markets, and to be called of men, Rabbi, Rabbi" (Matthew 23:5–7). High offices and worldly honors are not necessarily evil in and of themselves any more than money as an instrument of exchange is inherently evil. But just as the love of money corrupts and cankers the soul, so also does the love of praise and honor. Aspiring job-seekers today often lavish considerable time on the crafting of professional résumés, listing every achievement garnered in a person's lifetime— ironically little if any of which will count in Christ's measure of judgment. The same is true of callings and offices in the Church, which if used to "aspire to the honors of men" or to "gratify our pride, our vain ambition" incur only the displeasure of God (D&C 121:35, 37). No calling of any kind, from the least to the greatest, will assure a place in the kingdom of God.

Physical beauty or prowess will count as naught. "Beauty is vain," wrote Solomon (Proverbs 31:30), and physical beauty or strength assuredly will be of no worth at the Judgment. Pleasing physical attributes are largely the result of genetic inheritance, which renders any pride taken in them not only sinful, but somewhat ridiculous as well. The Lord also excoriates the vanity of fine clothing and jewelry in a lengthy passage in Isaiah: "Moreover the Lord saith, Because the daughters of Zion are haughty, and walk with stretched forth necks and wanton eyes, walking and mincing as they go" all of their ornaments, bracelets, headbands, earrings, rings, jewels, and "changeable suits of apparel," will be destroyed by calamities and "burning" (Isaiah 3:16–24). Modern revelation counsels the Saints of God to "let all thy garments be plain, and their beauty the beauty of the work of thine own hands" (D&C 42:40). He who had no beauty that we should desire him, who wore the plain apparel of a laborer all his life, will not be impressed by superficialities of flesh and fashion.

Worldly learning and wisdom, educational degrees and laurels, will count as naught. The Lord delights in his children learning truth and virtue. He has specifically commanded us to develop our talents and to "seek ye out of the best books words of wisdom" (D&C 88:118). Righteous learning, however, is ever graced by the spirit of God; it must never entail pride nor glorying in the wisdom of men. "If any man among you seemeth to be wise in this world, let him become a fool, that he may be wise. For the wisdom of this world is foolishness with God" (1 Corinthians 3:18–19). The Son of Man held no degrees and attended neither grammar school, rabbinical school, nor any university. He does not condemn learning, but those "who are puffed up because of their learning" (2 Nephi 9:42).

In short, *we will be stripped of all vain things.* Only by disregarding our worldly status and attainments can the Lord judge us independently of the circumstances of our birth and upbringing, and without regard to the vagaries of mortal life:

the fortunes or misfortunes encountered along the road. John Bunyan's classic work, *The Pilgrim's Progress*, speaks of a town called Vanity, wherein is located a great Fair that sells "all sorts of vanity," among them "Houses, Lands, Trades, Places, Honours, Preferments, Titles, Countr[ie]s, Kingdoms, Lusts, Pleasures, and Delights of all sorts."[12] The "Blessed One" had passed through the Fair centuries earlier and spent not a farthing on its wares. In like manner, we must shun the wares of Vanity Fair and repent of every desire thereof if we are to enter the kingdom of heaven. Nephi affirms this in his description of the final Judgment before the Keeper of the Gate: "And whoso knocketh, to him will he open; and the wise, and the learned, and they that are rich, who are puffed up because of their learning, and their wisdom, and their riches—yea, they are they whom he despiseth; and save they shall cast these things away, and consider themselves fools before God, and come down in the depths of humility, he will not open unto them" (2 Nephi 9:42). To "come down in the depths of humility" is what it means to have a broken heart and a contrite spirit, a heart purified of all desire for the wares of Vanity Fair.

Very well, if worldly attainments will not count in the final Judgment, what will? What words, thoughts, and actions will the Savior value?

My mission president, Rudolf K. Poecker, was one of the finest men I have ever known, a man of deep humility and overflowing love. On one occasion he asked a small group of missionaries where the Savior would go when he came to earth a second time. Hearing no answer, he smiled softly and offered his own: "I think he will visit Deseret Industries."

Deseret Industries is the Latter-day Saint version of Good

Will Industries. Along the Wasatch Front and throughout parts of Utah and other western states, it operates businesses that receive used goods and clothing donated by the public, which in turn are refurbished and sold. Sensing our skepticism about his answer, President Poecker, a former manager at the Industries, explained: "Who works at Deseret Industries? The blind, the deaf, the handicapped, the mentally impaired, the weak and humble of the earth. And among whom did Christ spend his ministry? Those very same persons of another era. So why would he not be found visiting and mingling with them again at his coming?"

President Poecker's question was only rhetorical, but his words have given me cause many times since that day to think about the Savior and what he truly values. I do not know if Christ literally will visit Deseret Industries when he comes again, and I do not think that the President meant to assert such, but it is certain that he will once again minister to the poor, the blind, the deaf, and the lowly. Similarly, at the Judgment Day he will care more about what we have done to bless our fellowman in quiet acts of service than all the worldly laurels we may have piled up.

In Amulek's famous discourse on the Atonement, the prophet begins by explaining the need for Christ's sacrifice and how it reconciles justice and mercy. The remainder of his discourse concerns repentance and our preparations to meet God. Amulek's words on repentance culminate with a powerful affirmation about the importance of service: "And now behold . . . after ye have done all these things, if ye turn away the needy, and the naked, and visit not the sick and afflicted, and impart of your substance, if ye have, to those who stand in need—I

141

say unto you, if ye do not any of these things, behold, your prayer is vain, and availeth you nothing, and ye are as hypocrites who do deny the faith. Therefore, if ye do not remember to be charitable, ye are as dross, which the refiners do cast out" (Alma 34:28–29). Charity, the pure love of Christ, is the virtue that Jesus will value most highly at the Day of Judgment. Paul and Mormon, writing on different continents and in different centuries, each extolled charity as the highest of all spiritual qualities, the one never-failing attribute of righteousness (Moroni 7; 1 Corinthians 13). In modern revelation, the Lord counsels, "And above all things, clothe yourselves with the bond of charity, as with a mantle, which is the bond of perfectness and peace" (D&C 88:125). Charity "preventeth a multitude of sins" (JST, 1 Peter 4:8) and will count more than any other virtue or work at the judgment seat, for "whoso is possessed of it at the last day, it shall be well with him" (Moroni 7:47).

Ancient Egyptian theology portrayed the final Judgment as a time when men's hearts would be weighed on a scale counterbalanced by only a feather. If the heart weighed more than the feather—if it was burdened in any way by worldly desires or pride—that man was doomed to destruction. Though non-Christian in origin, there is much truth in this conception. When every act is accounted for, the fundamental requirements fulfilled, and every covenant and ordinance validated—when all things are weighed in the balance—we will in the end be judged by the purity of our hearts. Outward obedience alone—what both Paul and Moroni called "dead works" (Hebrews 6:1; Moroni 8:23)—will not suffice to win entry into the kingdom of heaven.

Rather, "The Lord requireth the heart and a willing mind" (D&C 64:34).

This means that the Judgment Day will consist not so much of a summing up of assets and attainments, as a peeling away of all outward appearances to reveal the innermost self, that deep inner core of agency that ultimately defines who we are. Those who stand before Jesus with pure hearts—cleansed of worldly desires and wholly given to God—will be assured of crossing the veil into the kingdom of heaven. If such purity of heart seems remote, it may be comforting to remember that a pure heart does not come by one's own efforts alone. Rather, as we exercise our agency to come unto Christ in humility, he will cleanse our hearts of sin and purify our desires. The process of sanctification, as we read in the Book of Mormon, entails not so much the exertion of iron discipline as yielding the heart unto God (Helaman 3:35). The heirs of the celestial kingdom are not perfect in their own right, but rather are "just men *made perfect through Jesus* the mediator of the new covenant" (D&C 76:69; emphasis added).

As Moroni teaches, our hope is to become perfect in Christ: "Yea, come unto Christ, and be perfected in him, and deny yourselves of all ungodliness; and if ye shall deny yourselves of all ungodliness, and love God with all your might, mind and strength, then is his grace sufficient for you, that by his grace ye may be perfect in Christ" (Moroni 10:32). The grace of the Atonement makes possible not only the forgiveness of sins, but the perfecting of every attribute of righteousness. Hence, in Jesus Christ only can weak and fallen mortals become heirs of celestial glory. In the remarkable plan of God, our Judge is also our Advocate and Friend.

143

MERCY AND JUSTICE
IN THE DAY OF JUDGMENT

Life is patently unfair. Good men have bad things happen to them; evil men prosper, while the innocent suffer; liars and deceivers become rich; righteous men and women fall ill and die young; the worst sinners sometimes live to an old age. The manifest inequities of life have caused many persons to doubt the justice or even the existence of God; the injustice of life is still a major cause of agnosticism and atheism in the world today. The prophet Jeremiah struggled with the issue, crying out to the Lord: "Wherefore doth the way of the wicked prosper? wherefore are all they happy that deal very treacherously?" (Jeremiah 12:1).

When the disappointments and inequities of life are examined in isolation, this earthly probation may seem to be but one injustice after another, but when the time comes that we can view all things from a larger perspective—from the premortal life to the Day of Judgment—we will see that life in the long run, the eternal run, is altogether and perfectly just. God will not permit any injustice of mortal life to be perpetuated in the hereafter. Those who appear to have prospered in unrighteousness will discover that the dictates of justice are inviolable and inescapable. The righteous who have suffered injustices and loss will find that the story is not over: justice and mercy yet rule in the heavens. As Joseph Smith said, "All your losses will be made up to you in the resurrection, provided you continue faithful."[13]

The ministry of Christ is often contrasted with that of his friend and forerunner, John the Baptist, the last great prophet of the Mosaic dispensation. The austerity of John's life

144

personified the justice of the law and its unyielding strictness. Jesus by contrast brought tidings of a new law and a new dispensation, of a baptism by fire that would purify more surely than any ceremony or sacrifice of the Mosaic order. He bespoke mercy and love; he offered forgiveness and cleansing; he healed and made whole, both body and spirit. Yet it is important to understand that Christ's supernal love and mercy do not supplant justice, nor annul the authority of God's commandments. "I came not to send peace, but a sword" (Matthew 10:34), the Lord said, not only of his First Coming, but in prophetic token of his Second Coming, when with justice and judgment he will cleanse the earth of sin by fire.

When the last Judgment comes, those who have knowingly defied Christ's laws and rejected his gospel will discover the razor edge of his justice. The Lord spoke of those who will face condemnation at the judgment bar: "Then shall he say also unto them on the left hand, Depart from me, ye cursed, into everlasting fire, prepared for the devil and his angels . . . And these shall go away into everlasting punishment" (Matthew 25: 41, 46). What is more, the unrighteous will know with certitude that his judgment is true: "Then shall they confess, who live without God in the world, that the judgment of an everlasting punishment is just upon them" (Mosiah 27:31).

While it is reassuring to know that justice will prevail in the end of time, it is also sobering. Justice as an isolated principle is not nearly as salutary as it sounds, since perfect justice would consign us all to condemnation and spiritual death. While it is imperative that the injustice of mortal life be righted, it is equally imperative for man's eternal hopes that mercy counterbalance justice. To be judged by every idle word would be an impossible standard for all of us absent the possibility of repentance and forgiveness.

The acclaimed British film, *Winslow Boy*, portrays the true story of a protracted legal battle to clear the name of an innocent fourteen-year-old boy accused of theft at a military academy. The case goes to the highest courts of the land, including Parliament, before the lad is acquitted. When all is over, the boy's sister asks the defending attorney—normally a cold and calculating man—why he wept when the verdict was announced:

"I wept today because right had been done."

"Not justice?"

"No, not justice, right. Easy to do justice—very hard to do right."

It would be perfectly just for God to condemn this fallen world and reject its inhabitants as unworthy of his presence. But God does not only that which is just, but that which is right as well. "He is the Rock, his work is perfect: for all his ways are judgment . . . *just and right is he*" (Deuteronomy 32:4; emphasis added). Doing right means tempering justice with mercy, thus preparing a way for the salvation of his children.

The Atonement is what makes justice right. By invoking the power of mercy, it overpowers the decrees of justice in a way that does not violate ultimate justice. As Alma taught his son Corianton: "For behold, justice exerciseth all his demands, and also mercy claimeth all which is her own. . . . What, do ye suppose that mercy can rob justice? I say unto you, Nay; not one whit" (Alma 42:24–25). In the calculus of heaven, justice and mercy are two sides of an eternal continuum, neither of which can be disturbed or violated. The equilibrium between them is made possible by Christ's Atonement and death on the cross. By taking upon himself our sins, he met in full the demands of justice while, by the same redemptive act, opening the doors of mercy to the penitent.

The salvation thus made possible is a gift—a pure and simple gift—granted freely by a loving Father. "Salvation is free" (2 Nephi 2:4). By definition, mercy can be neither merited nor deserved. No amount of good works, no degree of virtue or righteousness, no claim of worthiness can save us without the grace of Christ. As Lehi taught, "by the law no flesh is justified; or, by the law men are cut off" (2 Nephi 2:5). Aaron, one of the sons of Mosiah, states this even more forcefully: "Since man had fallen *he could not merit anything of himself*; but the sufferings and death of Christ atone for their sins, through faith and repentance" (Alma 22:14; emphasis added).

This is why "it is by grace that we are saved, after all we can do" (2 Nephi 25:23). Divine grace is the dominant element of salvation, though ineffectual without human choice and effort. What does "all we can do" mean? It certainly does not mean perfect obedience, since no mortal achieves that; nor does it even really imply "doing our best," since no human being truly does his or her absolute best all of the time. "All we can do" simply means following the plain gospel road of exercising faith in the Savior, striving to keep the commandments, and repenting of sins whenever we fall short.[14] By following this path, the grace of Christ—his strength and spiritual sustenance—will accompany the sincere disciple of the Master each step of the way. Grace does not just cover the gap between our frailty and eventual perfection. Rather, it permeates the whole plan of salvation and is a daily gift from God:

"O to grace how great a debtor daily I'm constrained to be."[15] The eternal inheritance promised to the faithful is a gift of pure grace worth incalculably more than anything they could possibly merit on their own. By the infinite love of our Eternal Father, we will be "added upon . . . for ever and ever" (Abraham 3:26).

One manifestation of the supernal mercy of God is the fact that no individual will be judged or penalized by a law they were never taught. Those who knew not the fulness of the gospel in this life will hear it preached in the next and be given the opportunity to exercise faith in the Savior, to repent, and to receive the necessary ordinances by proxy. Nor will any individual be held accountable for actions beyond the scope of their agency—misdeeds caused by genetic disorders or mental disabilities; transgressions committed solely because of the false teaching and influence of parents; harmful acts done in involuntary reaction to situations of abuse or degradation, particularly when the latter occur in childhood and cripple a person's capacity to love or choose the right. The grace of Christ covers them all and more.

It is for this reason that we must never presume to pass judgment on the eternal fate of another human being nor look down on those who may be of an entirely different religion, culture, upbringing, or moral standard. We simply cannot know what forces and circumstances have shaped their lives, what handicaps they have faced, what teachings or cultural influences they have absorbed. Only the Almighty knows their hearts. Paul went about seeking to execute Christians: God looked into his soul and saw a chosen vessel. The Lamanites were bloodthirsty and idolatrous heathen: Alma and the sons of Mosiah recognized their divine worth and brought thousands to repentance; their children became the stripling warriors of Helaman. As the Lord told Samuel during his examination of the sons of Jesse, "the Lord seeth not as man seeth; for man looketh on the outward appearance, but the Lord looketh on the heart" (1 Samuel 16:7).

If we desire to partake of the mercy of Christ, he will expect us to show mercy toward our fellowman. The Lord explicitly commands us to forgive others their trespasses if we expect him to forgive ours (D&C 64:8–10). Otherwise, we would be like the unrighteous debtor in the Savior's parable who, having been forgiven of a ten-thousand-talent debt by his master, went out and cast a fellow servant into prison for failing to pay a mere hundred-pence debt (Matthew 18:23–35). If we expect Christ to remit our vast debts before him, we must first forgive the hundred-pence trespasses of our fellowman. If not—regardless of what injury they may have done to us—we will be found guilty of "the greater sin" (D&C 64:9). Here again, the Savior is our model, who said of his executioners, "Father, forgive them; for they know not what they do" (Luke 23:34).

The Prophet Joseph Smith spoke of God's mercy in a discourse to the Saints:

> But while one portion of the human race is judging and condemning the other without mercy, the Great Parent of the universe looks upon the whole of the human family with a fatherly care and paternal regard; He views them as His offspring. . . . He is a wise Lawgiver, and will judge all men, not according to the narrow, contracted notions of men, but, "according to the deeds done in the body whether they be good or evil," or whether

149

these deeds were done in England, America, Spain, Turkey, or India. He will judge them, "not according to what they have not, but according to what they have," those who have lived without law, will be judged without law, and those who have a law, will be judged by that law.[16]

The mercy of the Master transcends national lines, religious affiliations, and cultural boundaries and extends to the whole human race. He will never give up on any child of God, so long as the slightest hope of redemption remains, for "the worth of souls is great in the sight of God" (D&C 18:10).

THE PLEASING BAR OF THE GREAT JEHOVAH

The Book of Mormon opens with Nephi writing of his birth to goodly parents. The ancient testament thus begins where life begins, with the miracle of birth and parenthood. The very last verse of the Book of Mormon, by contrast, pertains to the Judgment Day, when ultimate accountability for mortal life takes place, the final curtain drops, and eternity commences. In Moroni's parting words to his readers, he portrays the Judgment as a day of triumph: "And now I bid unto all, farewell. I soon go to rest in the paradise of God, until my spirit and body shall again reunite, and I am brought forth triumphant through the air, to meet you before the pleasing bar of the great Jehovah, the Eternal Judge of both quick and dead" (Moroni 10:34).

The righteous, all who are on the Lord's side, need not fear the judgment of Christ. Though none will have lived a perfect life and all will rely on his grace, this God of perfect love will judge them with a tenderness unsurpassed. His words will delight, his judgments please, his "welcome home" touch the heart for eternity. Those who are chosen at that day will forever remember with joy "the pleasing bar" of the Great Jehovah. Following the judgment, they shall pass through the veil of eternity into the presence of God the Father and the hosts of heaven, never more to come out.

The phrase "pleasing bar" appears one other time in the scriptures, again associated with a farewell. It is the closing words of the prophet Jacob: "Finally, I bid you farewell, until I shall meet you before the pleasing bar of God, which bar striketh the wicked with awful dread and fear" (Jacob 6:13). The pleasing bar of judgment brings dread and fear to recalcitrant sinners. The fear thus mentioned is perhaps less fear of punishment than awareness of the eternal and irredeemable loss suffered by those who failed to heed the whisperings of the Spirit. For while they may eventually inherit a kingdom of glory, "where God and Christ dwell they cannot come, worlds without end" (D&C 76:112). Bruce C. Hafen has written of the poignant feelings of eternal loss he would feel if shut out from the gate of heaven: "What if, after having to turn away my head in shame from that eternal home, I were once again to hear the words [of the hymn] , 'Father, Mother, may I meet you . . . ?' I really don't think I could stand it. I would spend eternity trying to find some way of shutting off the pain of a longing that could not be fulfilled."[17] It is a compelling image of the irredeemable loss that the disobedient will reap at the Judgment Day.

At the pleasing bar of Christ, the judgments of the Lord will be so wondrously rendered, so absolutely right in every point that neither the righteous nor the unrighteous will be able to find the slightest flaw in their execution. All who stand before Jesus of Nazareth will know they have received exactly what justice is due them, have been given every conceivable mercy, and have been judged by a magistrate of perfect love. Joseph Smith distilled the singular perfection of that day into words that need no further elaboration: "When the designs of God shall be made manifest, and the curtain of futurity be withdrawn, we shall all of us eventually have to confess that *the Judge of all the earth has done right*."[18]

CHAPTER SEVEN

THE RETURN
OF THE KING

In the southeastern quadrant of the Aegean Sea, about thirty-seven miles from the ancient city of Miletus, lies Patmos, one of the Sporades Islands. Patmos is the place where John the Beloved saw a heavenly vision of the last days, recorded in the book of *Revelation*. The high point of John's vision is the return to earth of the Lord Jesus Christ:

"And I saw heaven opened, and behold a white horse; and he that sat upon him was called Faithful and True, and in righteousness he doth judge and make war.

"His eyes were as a flame of fire, and on his head were many crowns; and he had a name written, that no man knew, but he himself.

"And he was clothed with a vesture dipped in blood: and his name is called The Word of God. . . .

"And he hath on his vesture and on his thigh a name written, King of Kings, and Lord of Lords" (Revelation 19:11–13, 16).

When the Son of Man comes again to earth in his glory, he will come as Conqueror, as the King of Kings who will rule and reign for a thousand years.

The majesty of Christ's Second Coming as seen by John combines temporal elements—a white horse, fire, crowns, and a vesture dipped in blood—with the spiritual attributes epitomized by the Savior: faithfulness, truth, righteousness, and judgment. It is akin to the image of a conquering Messiah fixed in the minds of ancient Israel, an image that formed the expectations and hopes of the Jewish people for centuries, right up until the time that Jesus lived on earth. The Israelites of that day did not understand that the messianic prophecies of old pertained to both a first and a second advent of their King and intertwined elements of both.

Isaiah, for example, frequently mixed prophecies of Christ's mortal birth and life with prophecies of his Second Coming. "For unto us a child is born, unto us a son is given" (Isaiah 9:6), clearly refers to Christ's mortal birth, but the prophecy immediately subsequent that "the government shall be upon his shoulder" (v. 6) and that he will order and establish his kingdom upon the throne of David "henceforth even for ever" (v. 7) pertains to his later coming in glory. Similarly, Isaiah speaks of the political and temporal salvation of Israel, of God making "bare his holy arm in the eyes of all the nations" (Isaiah 52:10), then turns one chapter later to write of a Suffering Servant "despised and rejected of men" (Isaiah 53:3). Much of Isaiah 63 intermingles a vision of Christ's Second Coming with prophecies of his mortal life. Faced with such seemingly contradictory images and lacking inspired guidance, the scribes and rabbis of Israel fixated on the triumphal elements of Old Testament prophecy and hence were wholly unprepared for a Messiah who came to them as a carpenter from Nazareth. Learning and tradition proved stumbling blocks to enlightenment, while pride and envy led to their eventual rejection of the rightful King.

In his first coming, Christ was "the swordless king."[1] He neither sought nor exercised a particle of political or temporal power at any point of his ministry, but came instead to build a kingdom of God "within you" (Luke 17:21), a kingdom of the heart based on meekness, mercy, and love. One time in his ministry when the Savior "perceived that they would come and take him by force, to make him a king" (John 6:15), he quickly departed into the mountains alone, wanting nothing to do with it. "My kingdom is not of this world," he explained to Pilate. "If my kingdom were of this world, then would my servants fight, that I should not be delivered to the Jews: but now is my kingdom not from hence" (John 18:36). Instead of establishing an earthly dominion, he submitted to the powers of his day, even to their unjust verdict of death. Instead of liberating Israel from the bondage of Rome, he offered freedom from the bondage of sin. Even to his disciples, he made no promise of temporal deliverance, but only a promise that "I will not leave you comfortless: I will come to you" (John 14:18).

The fact that Christ did not exercise political power during his mortal ministry does not mean he intended his kingdom forever to be a spiritual kingdom only. Indeed, even while eschewing political power, he never denied his royal standing. When Pilate asked him point-blank, "Art thou the King of the Jews?" he answered in the quiet affirmative: "Thou sayest it" (Mark 15:2).[2] He was their rightful king by lineage and divine appointment, though he will assume the full rights of that office only upon his return in glory.

In an editorial in the *Times and Seasons* of July 15, 1842, Joseph Smith described the government of ancient Israel as a theocracy, with the Lord as its King, then added that only such a government could ever succeed in bringing permanent peace to the earth: "Other attempts to promote universal peace and happiness in the human family have proved abortive; every effort has failed; every plan and design has fallen to the ground; it needs the wisdom of God, the intelligence of God, and the power of God to accomplish this. The world has had a fair trial for six thousand years; the Lord will try the seventh thousand Himself."[3]

The Lord will try the seventh thousand years himself. When he comes for the second time, Immanuel will assume his rightful place as heir to the throne of David, Sovereign over a restored and reunified House of Israel. But this is not all. By virtue of his premortal station as Jehovah—Firstborn of the Father and Creator of the world—Christ will rule as a universal monarch over the whole earth, not only over Israel, but over the remnants of Gentile and heathen nations alike. He will establish a government that for the first time in world history will combine all legitimate temporal and spiritual authority in one. Following the trump of the seventh angel, as seen in John's vision, voices from heaven will announce that "the kingdoms of this world are become the kingdoms of our Lord, and of his Christ; and he shall reign for ever and ever" (Revelation 11:15).

The future reign of Christ as King resonates in sacred song, scripture, and prophetic voice. In the Latter-day Saint hymns alone, there are nearly forty distinct titles of Christ pertaining to his royal status:

The King of Angels	Our King, Our Deliverer, Our All
God the King	Our Savior, Lord, and King
King of Glory	The One Immortal King
Our God and King	Great King of Heaven
King of Israel	Our Maker, Lord, and King
Prince of Peace	The King and Blessed One
Redeemer King	Thou Good and Gracious King
The Newborn King	The Glorious King Immanuel
King of Creation	Heav'n's All-Gracious King
David's Royal Son	The Heav'n-Born Prince of Peace
Mighty King in Zion	Heav'nly King of Glory
Eternal King	Our King Forevermore
The Royal Master	Wondrous Sovereign of the Sea
Our Heavenly King	Prophet, Priest, and King
Christ the King	The Prince of Life
The King Eternal	The King of Kings
King Most High	Our Glorious King
King of Saints	The King Who Reigns in
Great God, Our King	Salem's Tower

A thoughtful reading of these titles, preferably aloud, con-veys the sense of worshipful reverence that mortal men and women ought to feel before the majesty of him whose right it is to reign. Such feelings are analogous in spirit to the honor and veneration that men have felt in the presence of great rulers throughout history, but immeasurably more powerful, because

Christ is not just another mortal king, but the veritable Lord of Lords and King of Kings.

In our day, when monarchy is a rare and largely discredited form of government and when political leaders, far from being worshiped, are often regarded with skepticism or disdain, we have largely forgotten what kings once meant to men. For all the failures of royal rule in Europe and elsewhere, the vision of a perfect human society thriving under a wise and virtuous ruler has held a powerful grip on mortal minds in many lands and across many centuries. Perhaps deeply ingrained in every human subconscious is an awareness of the reality of a Heavenly King—a kind of premortal imprint on the soul from which such yearnings stem. Given that a King indeed will rule the earth for a thousand years, it may be worthwhile to inquire as to the nature of monarchical government: its underlying principles, why it has so often failed in the past, and why it will truly and finally succeed only when a perfect being—a God himself—is King.

THE MEANING OF MONARCHY

Until the coming of the American and French Revolutions, the overwhelming consensus of learned opinion in Europe and elsewhere was that "monarchy was not simply the best possible form of government; it was almost the only conceivable form."[4] In ancient Greece, Plato had argued that the just society could be achieved only under the rule of a great philosopher-king, a man who would couple wisdom and political power in one. A similar vision of royal potential was revived and advanced in Renaissance Europe, culminating ultimately in the rise of the great kingdoms of the seventeenth and eighteenth centuries, the most splendid empires to have arisen since ancient times. The superiority of monarchy was thought to be its internal unity—by giving one man absolute power, strife, factionalism, and civil war could all be avoided. Rule by many was considered inherently unstable, since it was prone to division and conflict. The great English philosopher Thomas Hobbes pointed out that unlike unruly legislatures or the capricious masses of the people, a single man could not disagree with himself—hence, government by an absolute sovereign was the surest guarantor of indivisible government and a peaceful commonwealth.[5]

The most renowned and longest reigning of all the great European monarchs was Louis XIV of France, heralded as the Sun King. Assuming the crown at age five, this legendary ruler reigned for seventy-two years (1643–1715) over a kingdom that was the envy and fear of every other European realm. Employing nearly 30,000 craftsmen, Louis built the magnificent Palace of Versailles outside Paris, which remains today breathtaking in its expansiveness and beauty. At Versailles he established a royal court whose splendor and glory astounded all of Europe. So renowned was the French court that European rulers made it their model, and French became the predominant language of almost every palace on the continent. Louis presided over a great flowering of French arts and letters at home, as well as a buildup of French military power that made France the preponderant European land power, a status it did not relinquish until Napoleon's defeat at Waterloo, a full century after the Sun King's death.

At the pinnacle of his power, Louis XIV made the famous

claim, "I am the state," and in many respects he was just that. Life at the court and throughout the ranks of the French nobility revolved around the presence of the king. The power and importance of everyone and everything was measured by proximity to his person, with even his title of Sun King intimating that he was the center of the universe. It might be considered the greatest honor of a lifetime for a courtier to help dress the king in the morning or stand near him at a minor ceremony. The reverent treatment afforded the king of France was something we can hardly comprehend today, but it was integral to the notion of monarchy in his day. Men and women of the era literally worshiped their kings.

Yet for all the reverence and awe surrounding his personage, Louis XIV was a corrupt and profane man, subject to petty whims, divers lusts, and a famously bad temper. Though he ostensibly tried to do what was best for his kingdom, in his mind this meant primarily doing what was good for the ruling aristocracy, with little regard to the heavy burdens of taxation imposed on ordinary people. Whatever his accomplishments as a monarch, his personal life was marked by vice and excess, and the financial profligacy of his court and army paved the way for the monarchy's later bankruptcy and demise in the French Revolution. Measured against the longer-term historical consequences of his rule, Louis XIV must be judged a failure.

There were other kings and queens of European fame who could not match the splendor of the Versailles court, but whose lives were far more virtuous than that of the Sun King and who won the love and admiration of their people by their benevolence and generosity. There comes to mind the humble piety of Charles V of Hapsburg Spain; the benevolent reign of Elizabeth the Great of England; the saintly rule of Maria Theresa in Austria; the sterling virtue of Queen Victoria. Many of the kings and queens of Europe were despots, but many were fundamentally good of heart and worthy embodiments of Paul's saying, "the powers that be are ordained of God" (Romans 13:1).

Yet even the best of human beings have their flaws, and over the centuries the institution of monarchy became increasingly discredited by the vice, incompetence, and miscalculations of the continental monarchs. One-man rule simply did not work the way it was imagined. As commerce and technology advanced, and broader European society grew in education and wealth, monarchs were increasingly stripped of their powers until the few kings and queens that remain in Europe today are mere figureheads, holding no real power at all.

Monarchy as a governing institution ultimately failed for three reasons: first, because the monarchs had no underlying political legitimacy, no natural or constitutional right to govern. As awareness of individual rights grew, the defenders of monarchy were put on the defensive by a simple question: by what authority did one person, family, or dynasty claim to control the destinies of millions? The origins of the power of each royal house were shrouded in medieval darkness, often arising from obscure conquests hundreds of years earlier. Increasingly the "divine right" of kings to rule seemed dubious—even preposterous—before the rights of the people to govern their own lives democratically. Monarchy may have appeared to be of iron strength, but it stood on feet of clay, as Daniel had foreseen in prophecy (Daniel 2:33, 41–43).

The second glaring weakness of monarchy was that it entrusted the powers of the state—legislative, judicial, and executive—to one fallible person, often with few checks or balances against arbitrary rule or capricious decisions. The failure or success of the kingdom rested entirely on the wisdom and strength of a single human being, a person inevitably imperfect and unavoidably mortal. When a monarch was virtuous and strong, all might go well for a time; but when the wicked ruled, the people mourned. The latter, regrettably, proved more typical than the former. The problem was not just that Europe had bad luck with its kings. The problem, in the famous words of Lord Acton, was that "power corrupts and absolute power corrupts absolutely."[6] The very act of holding so much power in their hands inclined the hearts of monarchs toward despotism. The tendency of monarchy to concentrate corrupting power in one man was why Samuel warned the children of Israel against establishing a king (1 Samuel 8:10–18). Similar warnings were given—and similarly ignored—by the Jaredite and Nephite prophets to their people.[7] If it were possible to always have just and good men as kings, taught King Mosiah, then "it would be expedient that ye should always have kings to rule over you" (Mosiah 29:13). But because this was impossible, he counseled the people to select judges by popular vote instead.

Finally, the mortality of kings was the rub, as much as their imperfection. For even the finest of monarchs eventually died, exposing a third glaring weakness of monarchical rule: the problem of succession to the throne. The crown normally was transmitted by rigid laws of inheritance down to the closest heir by blood or marriage. Occasionally this pattern would elevate a better monarch to the throne. More often, it meant that any progress made by good monarchs was undermined by their being succeeded by incompetents, weaklings, moral degenerates, or tyrants. This pattern was precisely what led to disaster for the children of Israel in Egypt, when "there arose up a new king over Egypt, which knew not Joseph" (Exodus 1:8).

The slow and painful decline of monarchy did not erase the ancient dream of rule by a virtuous king. Among Christian peoples, at least, that dream increasingly became religious in content, focused on the promised reign of a heavenly king, a chosen heir to the throne of David, even the Lord Jesus Christ himself. The American colonists threw out, "God Save the King," but replaced it with an anthem of the same tune, ending with, "Great God, Our King!" If earthly kings were doomed to fail, a heavenly king could surely succeed. Such sentiments were particularly strong in the first part of the nineteenth century, when the Restoration took place.

This innate human yearning for a virtuous ruler and king, worthy of all acceptance and worship, will be fulfilled only when the Lord Jesus Christ returns in glory to establish for the first time a monarchy unsullied by the three fatal weaknesses described above. First, the rule of the Savior will be legitimate in every point, for he is the Creator of the earth and its divinely appointed Sovereign from before time and throughout the dispensations. Second, this monarch, like no other before, will be a being of perfect wisdom, knowledge, and virtue, in whom every trust can be placed and upon whose counsel and direction a perfect society can be established. Finally, the King will be immortal and hence require no successor: "Of the increase of his government and peace there shall be no end . . . from henceforth even for ever" (Isaiah 9:7).

In every point where royal government has failed in the past, it will find perfection in the reign of the King of Kings.

IN PREPARATION
FOR HIS COMING

An event so transcendent and epochal as the Second Coming will take place only after considerable prophetic foreshadowing and long preparation. In one sense, the whole history of the earth has been a preparatory period for his advent, which has been extolled by prophets in every dispensation. In the Old Testament alone, there are more than two dozen plain and distinct prophecies that speak of his latter-day coming, among the earliest recorded of which is the testimony of Job: "For I know that my redeemer liveth, and that he shall stand at the latter day upon the earth" (Job 19:25). The book of Isaiah and the Revelation of John both portray the history of the world as culminating in the return of the Lord to earth and the commencement of the great millennial reign.

The single most significant event preparatory to the Second Coming was the restoration of his Church and kingdom through the Prophet Joseph Smith in the early part of the nineteenth century. The Restoration brought back to earth all of the doctrines, authority, keys, ordinances, and covenants necessary for the salvation of God's children. It commenced "the rise of the Church of Christ in these last days" (D&C 20:1), both as an instrument of salvation and a vehicle to prepare the way for his return to earth. In a revelation given four years after the founding of the modern Church, the Lord commanded his servants to organize themselves and publish his words "for the purpose of building up my church and kingdom on the earth, *and to prepare my people for the time when I shall dwell with them*" (D&C 104:59; emphasis added).

The early Saints felt a deep spiritual yearning for the advent of the Lord, a yearning distilled in the words of a hymn by Parley P. Pratt:

Come, O thou King of Kings!
We've waited long for thee,
With healing in thy wings
To set thy people free.

Come, thou desire of nations, come;
Let Israel now be gathered home.[8]

Given their tremendous faith and vision, as well as the trials they faced, it was only natural that the first generation of Church members would look forward with particular longing for the Savior's advent, for a day of rest when the earth would enjoy its Sabbath.

What the Saints did not know, of course, was *when* the Lord would come. They knew only that the Church had been restored in the last days, that wars and rumors of wars were rampant, and that persecutions and troubles were on the increase. When Moses, Elias, and Elijah committed vital keys of the kingdom to Joseph Smith and Oliver Cowdery in the Kirtland Temple in April 1836, Elijah closed that glorious vision with these words: "Therefore, the keys of this dispensation are committed into your hands; and by this ye may know that the great and dreadful day of the Lord is near, even at the doors" (D&C 110:16). Reading this and other revelations, many early Church members came to believe that the Second Coming would be imminent, perhaps occuring even in their lifetime. The Prophet Joseph Smith himself was curious on this point. Late in his ministry, he sought the Lord "very earnestly to know the time of the coming of the Son of Man" (D&C 130:14), but he was given only an ambiguous answer and the instruction to "trouble me no more on this matter" (D&C 130:15).

During his life on earth, Christ taught regarding the time of his Second Coming, "But of that day and that hour knoweth no man, no, not the angels which are in heaven, neither the Son, but the Father" (Mark 13:32). The simple reality is that no human being has known or will know the time of Christ's coming, and all claims to the contrary are specious and all speculation about it idle. Nevertheless, modern-day revelation assures that we are living in the latter days of the world's history—a fact embodied in the very name of the Church—and we are specifically commanded to know the signs of the times and watch for his coming:

> Watch therefore, for ye know neither the day nor the hour wherein the Son of man cometh. (Matthew 25:13)

> If therefore thou shalt not watch, I will come on thee as a thief, and thou shalt not know what hour I will come upon thee. (Revelation 3:3)

> And the day cometh that you shall hear my voice and see me, and know that I am. Watch, therefore, that ye may be ready. (D&C 50:45–46)

> But the day soon cometh that ye shall see me, and know that I am; for the veil of darkness shall soon be

rent, and he that is not purified shall not abide the day. Wherefore, gird up your loins and be prepared. (D&C 38:8–9)

The time frame is not the main issue. Regardless of when the Lord may actually come, we are instructed to prepare to meet him *now*—now, because we know not the hour; now, because his coming is at the door; now, because at any time we may be taken from mortal life and called to stand before our Maker.

The Second Coming is described allegorically as the coming of the Bridegroom, an image used by the Savior in his parable of the foolish virgins. The Lord himself is the Bridegroom, and the establishment of Zion in the latter days is seen symbolically as the preparation of a bride to meet her Bridegroom (D&C 109:74). Members of the Church are specifically commanded to prepare for the wedding feast: "Wherefore, be faithful, praying always, having your lamps trimmed and burning, and oil with you, that you may be ready at the coming of the Bridegroom—For behold, verily, verily, I say unto you, that I come quickly" (D&C 33:17–18).

Those who prepare will "have received the truth, and have taken the Holy Spirit for their guide" (D&C 45:57), and they shall be counted among the wise virgins. Those who do not prepare will be found among the ranks of the foolish virgins, cast out from the wedding feast, with no late entry possible (Matthew 25:1–13).

Sometimes in our zeal to "be prepared," we focus exclusively on matters of temporal preparation: food storage, emergency preparedness, debt reduction, and the like. Vital and wise as these are, such preparations are primarily meant to fortify us against possible rainy days ahead, whether in the life of one family or individual, in times of national recession, or in the storms of the last days. But the preparation for the Lord's Coming as admonished in the scriptures must foremost be spiritual in nature, for his advent shall be an event of such intense glory that "he that is not purified shall not abide the day" (D&C 38:8). Without neglecting temporal preparedness, our highest preparations should always be of the heart: prayer, scripture study, righteous living, service to others, and obedience to the counsel of living prophets. Our circumstance as Latter-day Saints today is not dissimilar from that of the Nephite people prior to the coming of Christ, upon whom the Lord did "pour out his Spirit" in order "to prepare the minds of the children of men, or to prepare their hearts to receive the word which should be taught among them at the time of his coming" (Alma 16:16). We may fairly ask if our own minds and hearts are prepared for his coming.

THE DAWNING OF
A GLORIOUS DAY

The Restoration stands as a prelude, even a kind of crescendo, to the Second Coming of the Son of Man. The Prophet Joseph Smith wrote the following of the latter-day era that would culminate in the Lord's triumphal homecoming: "The building up of Zion is a cause that has interested the people of God in every age; it is a theme upon which prophets, priests and kings have dwelt with peculiar delight; they have looked forward with joyful anticipation to the day in which we live; and fired with heavenly and joyful anticipations they have sung and written and prophesied of this our day."[9] The establishment of Zion is the essential preliminary step to the return of the King Immanuel to earth.

Many Latter-day Saint hymns portray the Restoration as a dawn before the millennial day:

> *The day dawn is breaking, the world is awaking,*
> *The clouds of night's darkness are fleeing away.*
> *The worldwide commotion, from ocean to ocean,*
> *Now heralds the time of the beautiful day.*
>
> *Beautiful day of peace and rest,*
> *Bright be thy dawn from east to west.*
> *Hail to thine earliest welcome ray,*
> *Beautiful, bright millennial day.*[10]
>
> *Holding aloft our colors, we march in the glorious dawn.*[11]
>
> *The Morning Breaks, the shadows flee;*
> *Lo, Zion's standard is unfurled!*
> *The dawning of a brighter day, . . .*
> *Majestic rises on the world.*[12]

Dawn commences well before the sunrise. It begins with the appearance of a faint light in the east, a mere blush of the coming morning. As dawn progresses, the light grows brighter and brighter, extending westward until a warm radiance fills the sky. At last, in splendor, the sun rises over the horizon in the east, the brilliant celestial orb toward which the earth rolled throughout the night.

As with dawn, so it is with the Restoration of the gospel. It began as a faint light breaking forth in the eastern lands of the United States, a light noticed and heeded by few. But as the years and decades have passed, the light of the restored gospel has spread and extended throughout much of the earth. Yet all that has happened to the present is but a foretaste of what is to come. For as the dawn is followed by the sunrise, so also will the dawn of the Restoration be followed by the rising of the sun—the Son of God shining forth in the East in majesty. "For as the light of the morning cometh out of the east, and shineth even unto the west, and covereth the whole earth, so shall also the coming of the Son of Man be" (Joseph Smith—Matthew 1:26).

Isaiah prophesied, and modern revelation confirms, that the Lord will be clothed in glorious red apparel at the time of his coming: "Who is this that cometh down from God in heaven with dyed garments; yea, from the regions which are not known, clothed in his glorious apparel, traveling in the greatness of his strength? And he shall say: I am he who spake in righteousness, mighty to save. And the Lord shall be red in his apparel, and his garments like him that treadeth in the winevat" (D&C 133:46–48; see also Isaiah 63:1–2). The red apparel worn by the Savior at his Advent will symbolize the blood he shed at Gethsemane and Calvary in taking upon himself the sins of the world: "I have trodden the winepress alone; and of the people there was none with me: for I will tread them in mine anger, and trample them in my fury; and their blood shall be sprinkled upon my garments, and I will stain all my raiment" (Isaiah 63:3). In this manner, his Second Coming will bear witness to the Great Atonement wrought out by suffering during his first earthly sojourn in Palestine.

The rising of the Son of God in the east will be an event witnessed by all the nations of the earth: "Then shall appear the sign of the Son of Man in heaven, and then shall all the tribes of the earth mourn; and they shall see the Son of Man coming in the clouds of heaven, with power and great glory" (Joseph Smith—Matthew 1:36). The majesty of the Lord's appearance is likened to the unrolling of the heavens: "And there shall be silence in heaven for the space of half an hour; and immediately after shall the curtain of heaven be unfolded, as a scroll is unfolded after it is rolled up, and the face of the Lord shall be unveiled" (D&C 88:95). In the very moment when this happens, "the elements shall melt with fervent heat" (Mormon 9:2) as the earth is baptized by fire, much as it was baptized by water at the time of the flood in Noah's day. The Saints will be saved from the consuming fire that will accompany the Lord by being lifted up to meet him, along with many of the resurrected dead: "And the saints that are upon the earth, who are alive, shall be quickened and be caught up to meet him. And they who have slept in their graves shall come forth, for their graves shall be opened; and they also shall be caught up to meet him in the midst of the pillar of heaven" (D&C 88:96–97).

The prophet Joel refers to Christ's second advent as "the great and the terrible day of the Lord" (Joel 2:31), and Malachi uses the similar term, "the great and dreadful day" (Malachi 4:5). The events of that day will be great and marvelous to the righteous remnant of the Lord's people, and terrible and dreadful to the unbelieving and rebellious. The Lord will come to repossess a world awash in wickedness and strife and defaced by natural calamities. His coming will be a day of consuming destruction by fire. "Our God shall come, and shall not keep silence," says the psalmist. "A fire shall devour before him, and it shall be very tempestuous round about him" (Psalm 50:3).

Malachi prophesies that "the day cometh, that shall burn as an oven; and all the proud, yea, all that do wickedly, shall be stubble: and the day that cometh shall burn them up" (Malachi 4:1). The Lord in modern revelation vows vengeance upon the inhabitants of the earth, "a day of wrath, a day of burning, a day of desolation, of weeping, of mourning, and of lamentation" (D&C 112:24). The return of the King will be sudden and swift and will encompass the whole earth: "Then shall the arm of the Lord fall upon the nations. . . . And the Lord shall utter his voice, and all the ends of the earth shall hear it; and the nations of the earth shall mourn, and they that have laughed shall see their folly. And calamity shall cover the mocker, and the scorner shall be consumed; and they that have watched for iniquity shall be hewn down and cast into the fire" (D&C 45:47, 49–50).

While the righteous are watching for the coming of the Son of Man, among the wicked his advent will come without warning: "For yourselves know perfectly that the day of the Lord so cometh as a thief in the night. For when they shall say, Peace and safety; then sudden destruction cometh upon them, as travail upon a woman with child; and they shall not escape" (1 Thessalonians 5:2–3).

The destruction that will attend the Lord's advent will bring an abrupt end to the wars and conflict raging across the face of the earth on the last day of the last days. Isaiah foresaw the outcome in vision: "The Lord hath broken the staff of the wicked, and the sceptre of the rulers. . . . *The whole earth is at rest, and is quiet*" (Isaiah 14:5, 7; emphasis added). The sudden peace that will come upon the earth at the Savior's coming may be compared with Christ's calming of the Sea of Galilee

172

when he was aroused from slumber by his disciples. Then, a great storm threatened to destroy the disciples and their vessel until the Lord arose and declared, "Peace, be still" (Mark 4:39). Now, in the turmoil of the last days, the Lord's people will be threatened on every side by seeming destruction until the Savior appears and, at his command, wickedness is destroyed and peace ensues.

Isaiah writes that the surviving remnant, upon finding the earth at rest, will "break forth into singing" (Isaiah 14:7). In every quarter of the globe, the righteous will shout praises to the Lamb and raise their voices in a "New Song" unto Jesus Christ, the Lord. The singing of a New Song at the time of his coming is prophesied both in the Psalms and by Isaiah,[13] with the actual words of the song revealed in the Doctrine and Covenants, a portion of which reads as follows (the full text is found in the appendix):

> The earth hath travailed and brought forth her strength;
> And truth is established in her bowels;
> And the heavens have smiled upon her;
> And she is clothed with the glory of her God;
> *For he stands in the midst of his people.* (D&C 84:101; emphasis added)

The return of King Immanuel to stand in the midst of his people will mark a culminating moment in the Dispensation of the Fulness of Times, with all things gathered in one, Israel restored, and the Millennium ushered in. As he promised his disciples, the Savior will return to earth at the same place from which he ascended following his resurrection—on the crest of the Mount of Olives, east of Jerusalem. The Wedding Feast, the Great Supper of the Lamb, will commence, as Jesus drinks again "of the fruit of the vine" (D&C 27:5) with the resurrected prophets of old and with "all those whom my Father hath given me out of the world" (D&C 27:14).[14]

In Jerusalem, a tender reconciliation will take place between the Lord and his own cherished people, the remnant of Judah. His arrival in glory on the Mount of Olives will rescue the Jewish people from certain destruction in a great battle raging around Jerusalem. Then will come the moment of realization and reconciliation foreseen by Zechariah, when "they shall look upon me whom they have pierced, and they shall mourn for him, as one mourneth for his only son" (Zechariah 12:10). As Christ descends from the Mount of Olives to meet his people in Jerusalem, a sudden realization of who he is will spread among the people: "And then shall the Jews look upon me and say: What are these wounds in thine hands and in thy feet? Then shall they know that I am the Lord; for I will say unto them: These wounds are the wounds with which I was wounded in the house of my friends. I am he who was lifted up. I am Jesus that was crucified. I am the Son of God. And then shall they weep because of their iniquities; then shall they lament because they persecuted their king" (D&C 45:51–53). The shedding of tears will surely be mutual, as Jesus stands once again in his beloved Jerusalem, surrounded by the people of his own lineage, acknowledged as their Redeemer and King.

The magnificent events that will unfold in the immediate aftermath of the King Immanuel's coming are portrayed in the immeasurably beautiful words of Zechariah: "And his feet shall stand in that day upon the mount of Olives, which is before

Jerusalem on the east, and the mount of Olives shall cleave in the midst thereof. . . . And it shall come to pass in that day, that the light shall not be clear, nor dark: But it shall be one day which shall be known to the Lord, not day, nor night: but it shall come to pass, that at evening time it shall be light. And it shall be in that day, that living waters shall go out from Jerusalem; half of them toward the former sea, and half of them toward the hinder sea. . . . *And the Lord shall be king over all the earth*" (Zechariah 14:4, 6–9; emphasis added).

Preparatory to the Lord's coming, a temple shall be reared in Jerusalem, a restoration of the temple destroyed in 70 A.D. At his coming, as Zechariah prophesies, living waters shall flow forth from beneath that temple, rivers cascading downward from the heights of Jerusalem to the Dead Sea and the Mediterranean (the "former" and the "hinder" seas). Ezekiel foresaw that the river flowing forth from the temple in Jerusalem to the valley eastward would heal the saline waters of the Dead Sea, making it a living sea, full of life (Ezekiel 47:8).[15] As the Lord's dominion continues to unfold, Jerusalem shall be called a "city of truth" and a holy mountain (Zechariah 8:3), and sacred light shall fill its every precinct, as eventually even the bells of the horses in the city are inscribed with the words, "Holiness unto the Lord" (Zechariah 14:20). Across the earth, the Lord's people will inhabit and restore "the desolate cities" of the Gentiles (Isaiah 54:3), as a great work of reconstruction and restoration rolls forth. Joy and happiness will fill the hearts of people everywhere as the thousand-year reign of peace and truth begins, the reign of Jesus of Nazareth, the King of Kings.

THE SABBATH OF
THE MILLENNIAL DAY

"For the great Millennium, of which I have spoken by the mouth of my servants, shall come" (D&C 43:30). Holy writ divides the course of time into seven days of one thousand years each, making the last thousand years the Sabbath of the earth's creation: a time of peace, rest, and unparalleled spiritual outpouring. This prophetic calendar gives fresh meaning to one of the titles of Christ—*Lord of the Sabbath*—for he shall reign as Lord of the millennial day.

What will life be like during the Millennium? Although the details are not revealed, and the full splendor at present unimaginable, we do know the following:

It will be an era without conflict, enmity, or strife. "And in that day the enmity of man, and the enmity of beasts, yea, the enmity of all flesh, shall cease from before my face" (D&C 101:26). Universal peace will reign, and war will cease as swords are beaten into plowshares, and "nation shall not lift up sword against nation, neither shall they learn war any more" (Isaiah 2:4). Military laboratories and armories, weapons of mass destruction, diplomatic intrigue and machinations, conscription and regimentation for war—all shall pass away and cease to be centerpieces of human existence as they now are. The end of strife and conflict will not be confined only to the end of violence and war, but will also mean an end to political rivalries and factionalism, personal feuds and conspiracies, litigation and persecution, the conflict and clash of economic interests. Societies today squander huge amounts of energy and capital in conflict and division of every kind. In the millennial day, the energies of God's children will be channeled in divinely guided cooperation toward righteous ends.

The adversary will be bound, unable to tempt God's children. "And in that day Satan shall not have power to tempt any man" (D&C 101:28). John the Revelator portrays the binding of Satan in stark language: "And I saw an angel come down from heaven, having the key of the bottomless pit and a great chain in his hand. And he laid hold on the dragon, that old serpent, which is the Devil, and Satan, and bound him a thousand years, and cast him into the bottomless pit, and shut him up, and set a seal upon him, that he should deceive the nations no more, till the thousand years should be fulfilled" (Revelation 20:1–3). In such felicitous circumstances, "children shall grow up without sin unto salvation" (D&C 45:58), living righteously from the day of accountability to the end of mortality. Difficult as it is for us to imagine a world without sin, this will be among the sweetest fruits of the Millennium.

Economic inequality will cease, and there will be no poor among them. For the first time since Enoch, an economic order will reign in which mankind is "united according to the union required by the law of the celestial kingdom" (D&C 105:4). Division of property and selfish interests will not prevail, but wealth will be regarded as the common inheritance of all God's children. All the vices associated with division of property—avarice, pride, covetousness, envy, inequality, and selfishness—will pass away. No longer will the poor of the earth be downtrodden or despised—rather, all will be lifted up and made as one in a society of true brotherhood and love. In a powerful prophecy in the Doctrine and Covenants, the Lord describes the great wedding feast that will occur at his coming as "a supper of the house of the Lord . . . unto which all nations shall be invited" (D&C 58:9) including the rich and learned and great ones of the earth. But he adds pointedly: "*And after that cometh the day of my power;* then shall the poor, the lame, and the blind, and the deaf, come in unto the marriage of the Lamb, and partake of the supper of the Lord" (D&C 58:11; emphasis added). The first shall be last and the last first when the great Captain of the Poor comes to rule.

It will be an era of unprecedented revelation and enlightenment, indeed "a time to come in the which *nothing* shall be withheld" (D&C 121:28). The veil will be exceedingly thin, and the floodgates of divine revelation wide open. "Yea, verily I say unto you, in that day when the Lord shall come, he shall reveal all things . . . things most precious, things that are above, and things that are beneath, things that are in the earth, and upon the earth, and in heaven" (D&C 101:32, 34). In a world filled with the light of Christ, we can anticipate a great flowering of art, literature, and music; a quantum increase in scientific understanding of every kind; mastery of the natural elements and their harnessing for good; dramatic increases in agricultural and manufacturing productivity; unparalleled works of architecture, design, and beauty. Righteousness and truth will "sweep the earth as with a flood" (Moses 7:62) and millions upon millions of God's children will flock to the banner of Christ. Not every person who lives on earth during the Millennium—and certainly not in its beginning—will be a member of the Church, for we are told that heathen nations will continue after his coming (D&C 45:54; Zechariah 14:17–18). Even those who are not of the covenant, however, will bow to the rod of Christ and submit to his rule. This will be the condition, at least, at the beginning of the Millennium. But as Joseph Fielding Smith observed: "The gospel will be taught far more intensely and with greater power during the millennium until all the inhabitants of the earth shall embrace it."[16] The redemption of the deceased will also proceed apace, as a mighty work of building temples and performing ordinance work will move across the face of the earth. The light of Christ will draw all nations unto him until the time comes that "the earth shall be full of the knowledge of the Lord, as the waters cover the sea" (Isaiah 11:9).

Death as we now know it will no longer exist. This does not mean that the millennial inhabitants of earth will be literally immortal, but rather: "In that day an infant shall not die until he is old; and his life shall be as the age of a tree; and when he dies he shall not sleep, that is to say in the earth, but shall be changed in the twinkling of an eye, and shall be caught up, and his rest shall be glorious" (D&C 101:30–31). The earth will be "renewed and receive its paradisiacal glory" (Articles of Faith 10), entering a new phase of its existence, more terrestrial than telestial in nature. In such a higher state, bodily disease, mental illness, and many of the degenerative tendencies of biological life will cease or at least be greatly diminished in effect. Flesh will no longer have need to consume flesh, making it literally possible for a lion to lie down with a lamb.

The face of the earth will experience great physical transformations. In the miraculous cleansing by fire that will take place at the time of the Savior's coming, "the earth shall be transfigured" (D&C 63:21). As Isaiah prophesied: "Every valley shall be exalted, and every mountain and hill shall be made low: and the crooked shall be made straight, and the rough places plain: and the glory of the Lord shall be revealed, and all flesh shall see it together" (Isaiah 40:4–5). Similar language is used in the Book of Mormon to describe the geological upheavals that occurred in the New World at the time of the Savior's death, but in that instance, the changes were confined to a portion of the earth; at his Second Coming, the whole planet will be affected. "He shall command the great deep, and it shall be driven back into the north countries, and the islands shall become one land; and the land of Jerusalem and the land of Zion shall be turned back into their own place, and the earth shall be like as it was in the days before it was divided" (D&C 133:23–24).

Christ will reign personally upon the earth, in the words of the tenth Article of Faith. The grandeur of that era will unfold under the watchful eye of Jesus Christ, its divine Sovereign, while human ego, pride, and selfishness will play no role whatever in the governance of world affairs, for "ye shall have no laws but my laws when I come" (D&C 38:22). He will make the earth his dwelling place as, at long last, the government rests upon the shoulder of him whose right it is to reign, "For the Lord shall be in their midst, and his glory shall be upon them, and he will be their king and their lawgiver" (D&C 45:59). The Savior will govern the earth from two great world capitals, one in old Jerusalem, the other at New Jerusalem on the American continent: "For out of Zion shall go forth the law, and the word of the Lord from Jerusalem" (Isaiah 2:3).

The King of Kings will be no caretaker ruler or absentee landlord, but a loving and personal Lord, who in tender portent of those days has said, "I will be your king and watch over you" (D&C 38:21). As during his days in Palestine, he will again receive little children, give blessings to his people, teach, counsel, and direct. The earth will be his realm, and all the pure in heart who enter his holy temple will see him there (D&C 97:16). By his power and presence, and only thereby, will the glory of the Millennium be possible at all.

In 1982, I visited Jerusalem for the first time. I was alone on business and on the first evening walked through the stone walls of the Old City and made my way along the southern and eastern edges of the wall until the Mount of Olives and the Garden of Gethsemane were in view. It was a moment of quiet reverence and contemplation. I lingered a long time until it was quite dark, then made my way back to the hotel through the Old City. It was a warm evening in May, and I passed a group of young boys and girls playing happily together in the streets. Their carefree innocence touched my heart. Upon arriving back in my room, I opened the Old Testament randomly and, to my surprise, came upon a prophecy of Zechariah regarding the city of Jerusalem in the millennial day: "And the streets of the city shall be full of boys and girls playing in the streets thereof" (Zechariah 8:5). That verse for me has ever since personified the joy and peace of the earth's Sabbath Day—a time to come in which children will grow up free from fear, from neglect and abuse, from darkness and ignorance; a time in which the little ones of the world will live under the seal of a higher law and a loving Lord. I yearn for the day when in every village and city of the world, boys and girls will play in innocence, and every child know the peace of a happy home. For me, that is the Millennium.

THE KING OF KINGS FOREVER

The Sabbath reign of the King of Kings will constitute the crowning era of the history of the earth, prior to its resurrection in celestial glory. But the conclusion of the Millennium will not end the work of Jesus Christ, who will continue to reign under the Eternal Father as a Heavenly Sovereign forever. When "a new heaven and a new earth" (Revelations 21:1) arise in place of the old, when the earth is glorified and enters its "sanctified, immortal, and eternal state" (D&C 77:1), Immanuel will remain our Lord and God. All who inherit celestial glory will be of the church of the Firstborn (D&C 76:54) and "shall dwell in the presence of God and his Christ forever and ever" (D&C 76:62).

The Apostle John beheld a vision of the heavenly New Jerusalem, the City of God, which he described in language as exalted as any found in holy writ:

"And the twelve gates were twelve pearls; every several gate was of one pearl: and the street of the city was pure gold, as it were transparent glass.

"And I saw no temple therein: for the Lord God Almighty and the Lamb are the temple of it.

"And the city had no need of the sun, neither of the moon, to shine in it: for the glory of God did lighten it, and the Lamb is the light thereof. . . .

"And he shewed me a pure river of water of life, clear as crystal, proceeding out of the throne of God and of the Lamb.

"In the midst of the street of it, and on either side of the river, was there the tree of life, which bare twelve manner of fruits, and yielded her fruit every month: and the leaves of the tree were for the healing of the nations" (Revelations 21:21–23; 22:1–2).

Neither sun nor moon nor stars, nor even the light of temples, are needed to illuminate the celestial realm. God the Father and Jesus Christ are the light thereof: light everlasting, light divine. From eternity to eternity, and kingdom upon kingdom, shall they reign. All the children of the Father who come unto Christ and are perfected in him will be made joint-heirs of eternal life, inheriting "thrones, kingdoms, principalities, and powers, dominions, all heights and depths" (D&C 132:19). Jesus of Nazareth, who bore our sins and carried our sorrows, will make of the redeemed, with him, kings and queens in realms on high.

Thy Kingdom come. Thy will be done. And may glory, honor, and power be to the King of Kings, forever.

THE NEW SONG

The Lord hath brought again Zion;
The Lord hath redeemed his people, Israel,
According to the election of grace,
Which was brought to pass by the faith
And covenant of their fathers.

The Lord hath redeemed his people;
And Satan is bound and time is no longer.
The Lord hath gathered all things in one.
The Lord hath brought down Zion from above.
The Lord hath brought up Zion from beneath.

The earth hath travailed and brought forth her strength;
And truth is established in her bowels;
And the heavens have smiled upon her;
And she is clothed with the glory of her God;
For he stands in the midst of his people.

Glory, and honor, and power, and might,
Be ascribed to our God; for he is full of mercy,
Justice, grace and truth, and peace,
Forever and ever, Amen.

(D&C 84:99–102)

NOTES

NOTES TO CHAPTER 1

Because Chapter 1 is a letter, I chose not to place any notes in it. The sources used include:

Page 2, commentary from a seminary teacher and writer—Carl H. Jacob, *While of These Emblems . . .* (Salt Lake City: Deseret Book Co., 1962), 177–179.

Page 4, quotation from Joseph Smith—Joseph Smith, *Teachings of the Prophet Joseph Smith*, sel. Joseph Fielding Smith (Salt Lake City: Deseret Book, 1976), 379.

Page 9, statement by President David O. McKay—in Conference Report, October 1956, 6.

Page 10, reference to children's book—Lois Lowry, *The Giver*, Boston: Houghton Mifflin, 1993.

Page 14, letter from President McKay to his son—Clare Middlemiss comp., *Treasures of Life* (Salt Lake City: Deseret Book Co., 1962), 275–78.

NOTES TO CHAPTER 2

1. "O Come, O Come, Emmanuel," in Henry W. Simon, ed., *A Treasury of Christmas Songs and Carols* (Boston: Houghton Mifflin, 1955), 134–35. I have altered the spelling of Emmanuel to Immanuel to be consistent with other usages. I have also changed the translation of the last line of the fifth stanza to more accurately reflect the original Latin.

2. "O God, the Eternal Father," *Hymns* (Salt Lake City: The Church of Jesus Christ of Latter-day Saints, 1985), no. 175.

3. "Once in Royal David's City," *Hymns*, no. 205.

4. Alfred Edersheim, *The Life and Times of Jesus the Messiah* (Peabody, Mass.: Hendrickson Publishers, 1993), 131–32.

5. Joachim Jeremias, *Jerusalem in the Time of Jesus*, trans. F. H. and C. H. Cave (Philadelphia: Fortress Press, 1969), 76.

6. A very ancient Christian tradition—dating back as early as the 1st century A.D.—purports that Christ was born in a limestone cave.

7. Matthew Hale, "I Have a Room," in Calvin Miller, ed., *The Book of Jesus:*

A Treasury of the Greatest Stories and Writings about Christ (New York: Simon & Schuster, 1996), 124.

8. On Christ as the heir of David's throne and the Second David, see Bruce R. McConkie, *The Promised Messiah* (Salt Lake City: Deseret Book Co., 1978), 185–96, and Bruce R. McConkie, *The Millennial Messiah* (Salt Lake City: Deseret Book Co., 1982), 589–611.

9. Bruce R. McConkie, *Doctrinal New Testament Commentary*, 3 vols. (Salt Lake City: Bookcraft, 1965), 1:85.

10. Charles Dickens, *A Christmas Carol* (London: Penguin Books, 1946), 137.

11. Ibid., 138.

12. Ibid., 95.

13. Gordon B. Hinckley, First Presidency Christmas Devotional, December 3, 1995. See also "Warm Messages, Festive Setting," *Church News*, December 9, 1995.

14. Neal A. Maxwell, as quoted in "Sparkling Lights Are Symbols of Greater, Glorious Divine Light," *Church News*, December 6, 1997, 3.

15. Ibid.

16. Christina Rossetti, "In the Bleak Mid-Winter," cited in Calvin Miller, ed. *The Book of Jesus*, 147.

17. Joseph Smith, *History of the Church*, 6:134–35.

18. "Joy to the World," *Hymns*, no. 201.

NOTES TO CHAPTER 3

1. "Thy Will, O Lord, Be Done," *Hymns* (Salt Lake City: The Church of Jesus Christ of Latter-day Saints, 1985), no. 188.

2. "Jesus, Once of Humble Birth," *Hymns*, no. 196.

3. Mark Twain, *The Prince and the Pauper* (New York: Bantam Books, 1991), 12.

4. Ibid.

5. W. Dyer, as quoted in John Blanchard, "A Symposium on Jesus' Identity," in Calvin Miller, ed., *The Book of Jesus: A Treasury of the Greatest Stories and Writings about Christ* (New York: Simon & Schuster, 1996), 55.

6. Leona B. Gates, "In His Steps," in *Best Loved Poems of the LDS People*, ed. Jack M. Lyon, Linda Ririe Gundry, Jay A. Parry, and Devan Jensen (Salt Lake City: Deseret Book Co., 1996), 179.

7. Pamela Hamblin, previously unpublished. Used by permission.

8. On this point, see also 2 Nephi 2:8, 10:24, 25:23, 31:19; Helaman 14:13; Moroni 6:4; D&C 3:20; Ephesians 2:8; 2 Timothy 1:9.

9. Neal A. Maxwell, *Not My Will, But Thine* (Salt Lake City: Bookcraft, 1988), 51. See also the thoughtful discussion in Vaughn J. Featherstone, *The Incomparable Christ* (Salt Lake City: Deseret Book Co., 1995), 7–14.

10. Jeffrey R. Holland, *Christ and the New Covenant: The Messianic Message of the Book of Mormon* (Salt Lake City: Deseret Book Co., 1997), p. 343.

11. "O Holy Night," in Henry W. Simon, ed., *A Treasury of Christmas Songs and Carols* (Boston: Houghton Mifflin, 1955), 197–200.

NOTES TO CHAPTER 4

1. Charles Edward Jefferson, *The Character of Jesus*, New York: Thomas Y. Cromwell, 1908.

2. Matthew 13:55 renders this "Is not this the carpenter's son?" Because of this verse, many have asserted that we know only the occupation of Joseph with certainty, though it may be logical to presume that Jesus followed in his footsteps and was his apprentice. The verse in Mark, however, confirms that Christ too was a carpenter and known as such among his people.

3. Saint Bonaventura, as quoted in Frederic W. Farrar, *The Life of Christ* (Salt Lake City: Bookcraft, 1994 [1875]), 95.

4. Frederic W. Farrar, in ibid., 87–89.

5. Bruce Barton, *The Man Nobody Knows* (Indianapolis, IN: The Bobbs-Merrill Co., 1952), 43. I recommend Barton's entire chapter, entitled, "The Outdoor Man."

6. Bruce Barton, *The Man Nobody Knows*, 53. See also p. 52 on his popular standing in Judaean society.

7. Joseph Smith, *Teachings of the Prophet Joseph Smith*, sel. Joseph Fielding Smith (Salt Lake City: Deseret Book Co., 1976), 270.

8. See also Luke 6:19, where virtue goes from him to heal the multitudes.

9. Charles Edward Jefferson, *The Character of Jesus*, 343.

10. Charles Lamb, as cited in ibid., 341.

NOTES TO CHAPTER 5

1. "Dear to the Heart of the Shepherd," *Hymns* (Salt Lake City: The Church of Jesus Christ of Latter-day Saints, 1985), no. 221.

2. I am indebted to Dr. Truman G. Madsen's essay for some of the insights noted here. For a fuller account of the symbolism of the olive press, see Truman G. Madsen, "The Olive Press: A Symbol of Christ," in Stephen D. Ricks and John W. Welch, eds., *The Allegory of the Olive Tree: The Olive, the Bible, and Jacob 5* (Salt Lake City: Deseret Book Co., 1994) 1–10.

3. The accounts of the New Testament evangelists are found in Matthew 26:36–46; Mark 14:26–42; Luke 22:39–46; and John 18:1.

4. James E. Talmage, *Jesus the Christ* (Salt Lake City: Deseret Book Co., 1982), 568.

5. As the *Bible Dictionary* observes, under "Angels," the term angels normally refers to "those ministering persons who have a body of flesh and bone, being either resurrected from the dead (reembodied), or else translated." However,

189

it can also refer to ministering spirits, mortal messengers of God, or those saved in the celestial kingdom, but not exalted. Since there was no resurrection prior to Christ, and since "there are no angels who minister to this earth but those who do belong or have belonged to it" (D&C 130:5), the angel who ministered to the Savior in Gethsemane cannot have been a resurrected being.

6. Bruce R. McConkie, *The Mortal Messiah*, 4 vols (Salt Lake City: Deseret Book Co., 1981), 4:124–128.

7. Lucy Mack Smith, *History of Joseph Smith by His Mother* (Salt Lake City: Bookcraft, 1954), 132.

8. Ezra Taft Benson, *The Teachings of Ezra Taft Benson* (Salt Lake City: Bookcraft, 1988), 14.

9. For further definition of spiritual death see 2 Nephi 9:12; Alma 42:9; Helaman 14:16.

10. Frederic W. Farrar, *The Life of Christ*, (Salt Lake City: Bookcraft, 1994 [1875]), 588.

11. James Talmage, *Jesus the Christ*, 598–601. See also a summary of recent scholarly opinion on the issue in Richard Neitzel Holzapfel, *A Lively Hope* (Salt Lake City: Bookcraft, 1999), 44–45.

12. James Talmage, *Jesus the Christ*, 590.

13. The exact place of the Crucifixion is not known, of course. The arguments in favor of a site near the Damascus Gate are set forth in part by General Charles Gordon in the appendix of John Wilkinson, *Jerusalem As Jesus Knew It: Archaeology as Evidence* (London: Thames and Hudson, 1978), 198–200. See also 146–47, including Illustration 101 on p. 147.

14. The preceding three verses clearly refer to an heir to the throne of David to whom belongs the rights of government and who is "father to the inhabitants of Jerusalem."

15. John Wilkinson, *Jerusalem As Jesus Knew It*, 154. See also Bruce R. McConkie, *The Mortal Messiah*, 4:215, footnote 4.

16. James Talmage, *Jesus the Christ*, 607–14; Frederic W. Farrar, *The Life of Christ*, 640–41; John Wilkinson, *Jerusalem As Jesus Knew It*, 151–55; William D. Edwards, Wesley J. Gabel, and Floyd E. Hosmer, "On the Physical Death of Jesus Christ," *JAMA*, March 21, 1986, 1455–63.

17. Psalm 86 is not normally identified as a Messianic psalm, for it is a prayer of David. Yet it may also be read as a prayer of Christ; this is particularly true of the last five verses.

18. "O Savior, Thou Who Wearest a Crown," *Hymns*, no. 197.

19. James E. Talmage, *Jesus the Christ*, 612–13.

20. Ibid., 615.

NOTES TO CHAPTER 6

1. Flannery O'Connor, "Revelation," in Flannery O'Connor, *The Complete Stories* (New York: Farrar, Straus and Giroux, 1946 [1971]), 491.
2. Ibid., 506–7.
3. Ibid., 508.
4. William Barclay, *Jesus As They Saw Him: New Testament Interpretations of Jesus,* (New York: Harper & Row Publishers, 1962), 296–98.
5. Most of this list comes from Barclay, *op. cit.* I have added the last four parables to his list.
6. See also John 5:27: "[The Father] hath given him authority to execute judgment also, because he is the Son of man."
7. Obviously Judas will not be one of them. Perhaps the man who succeeded him in the ranks of the Twelve, Matthias, will assume his place.
8. The prophet Mormon taught this doctrine as follows: "And I write also unto the remnant of this people, who shall also be judged by the twelve whom Jesus chose in this land; and they shall be judged by the other twelve whom Jesus chose in the land of Jerusalem" (Mormon 3:19).
9. The involvement of other priesthood leaders in the judgment is suggested in D&C 20:13.
10. See also 2 Nephi 9:15: "And it shall come to pass that when all men shall have passed from this first death . . . they must appear before the judgment-seat of the Holy One of Israel."
11. Victor Hugo, *Les Misérables,* London: Penguin Books, 1982.
12. John Bunyan, *The Pilgrim's Progress* (Oxford: Oxford University Press, 1966), 73.
13. Joseph Smith, *Teachings of the Prophet Joseph Smith,* sel. Joseph Fielding Smith (Salt Lake City: Deseret Book Co., 1976), 296.
14. See, for example, Alma 24:11. I am indebted to Stephen Robinson for pointing out this scripture to me.
15. "Come Thou Fount of Every Blessing," *Hymns,* (Salt Lake City: The Church of Jesus Christ of Latter-day Saints, 1948), no. 70.
16. Joseph Smith, *Teachings of the Prophet Joseph Smith,* 218.
17. Bruce C. Hafen, *The Broken Heart* (Salt Lake City: Deseret Book Co., 1989), 88.
18. Joseph Smith, *Teachings of the Prophet Joseph Smith,* 218; emphasis added.

NOTES TO CHAPTER 7

1. William Barclay, *Jesus As They Saw Him: New Testament Interpretations of Jesus* (New York: Harper & Row Publishers, 1962), 244.
2. This exchange is recorded in almost identical language in all four of the Gospels. See Matthew 27:11; Mark15:2; Luke 23:3; John 18:37.

3. Joseph Smith, *Teachings of the Prophet Joseph Smith*, sel. Joseph Fielding Smith (Salt Lake City: Deseret Book Co., 1976), 252.

4. Bernard Guenée, *States and Rulers in Later Medieval Europe*, trans. Juliet Vale (London: Basil Blackwell, 1985), 67.

5. Thomas Hobbes, *Leviathan* (New York: Collier Books, 1962), 139–44.

6. John Emerich Edward Dalberg Acton, *Letter to Bishop Mandell Creighton*, April 5, 1887, as cited in John Bartlett *Familiar Quotations*, 14th ed. (Boston: Little, Brown and Company, 1968), 750.

7. Ether 6:23; 2 Nephi 5:18; Mosiah 29:16–25.

8. "Come, O Thou King of Kings," *Hymns* (Salt Lake City: The Church of Jesus Christ of Latter-day Saints, 1985), no. 59.

9. Joseph Smith, *Teachings of the Prophet Joseph Smith*, 231.

10. "The Day Dawn Is Breaking," *Hymns*, no. 52.

11. "Carry On," *Hymns*, no. 255.

12. "The Morning Breaks," *Hymns*, no. 1.

13. Psalms 96:1, 98:1, and 149:1; Isaiah 42:10.

14. The Savior prophesied of this event at the time of the sacrament of the Last Supper: "For I say unto you, I will not drink of the fruit of the vine, until the kingdom of God shall come" (Luke 22:18; see also Matthew 26:29; Mark 14:25).

15. Joseph Smith, *Teachings of the Prophet Joseph Smith*, 286–87.

16. Joseph Fielding Smith, *Answers to Gospel Questions*, 5 vols. (Salt Lake City: Deseret Book Co., 1957), 1:110–11.

INDEX